‖‖‖ ‖ ‖‖‖‖‖‖ ‖ ‖ ‖‖ ‖‖‖‖‖‖‖‖‖‖‖‖ ‖‖ ‖‖

W9-AXO-255

Judy E. Pickens has been a communication consultant since 1978, and works out of her home in Seattle, Washington, for a variety of clients. This book is a compilation of her experiences as both a buyer and seller of freelance services.

A GIFT FROM
ADVENTIST DEVELOPMENT
AND RELIEF AGENCY
P O BOX 60808 - WASH, DC 20039
IN COOPERATION WITH THE PUBLISHER
NOT TO BE SOLD

A GIFT FROM
ADVENTIST DEVELOPMENT
AND RELIEF AGENCY
IN COOPERATION WITH THE PUBLISHER
NOT TO BE SOLD

THE FREE-LANCER'S HAND-BOOK

A COMPREHENSIVE
GUIDE TO
SELLING YOUR
FREELANCE SERVICES

NOT FOR RESALE

JUDY E. PICKENS

PRENTICE-HALL, INC. A SPECTRUM BOOK Englewood Cliffs, N.J. 07632

Library of Congress Cataloging in Publication Data

Pickens, Judy E.
    The freelancer's handbook.

    (A Spectrum Book)
    Includes index.
    1. Self-employed—Handbooks, manuals, etc.
2. Consultants—Handbooks, manuals, etc. I. Title.
HD8036.P5   658.8'5   81-10636
                     AACR2

ISBN 0-13-330688-7 {PBK}
ISBN 0-13-330696-8

This Spectrum Book is available to businesses and organizations at a special discount when ordered in large quantities. For information, contact Prentice-Hall, Inc., General Book Marketing, Special Sales Division, Englewood Cliffs, N.J. 07632.

© 1981 by Judy E. Pickens

A SPECTRUM BOOK

All rights reserved. No part of this book
may be reproduced in any form or by any means
without permission in writing from the publisher.

10 9 8 7 6 5 4 3 2 1

Printed in the United States of America

Editorial production/supervision and interior design by Cyndy Lyle Rymer
Manufacturing buyer: Cathie Lenard
Cover Design by Judith Kazdym Leeds

Prentice-Hall International, Inc., *London*
Prentice-Hall of Australia Pty. Limited, *Sydney*
Prentice-Hall of Canada, Ltd., *Toronto*
Prentice-Hall of India Private Limited, *New Delhi*
Prentice-Hall of Japan, Inc., *Tokyo*
Prentice-Hall of Southeast Asia Pte. Ltd., *Singapore*
Whitehall Books Limited, *Wellington, New Zealand*

Contents

Preface   vii

1 Is Freelancing for You?   1

What "Freelance" Means, 2 / Why People Freelance, 5 / The
Drawbacks of Freelancing, 9 / What Do *You* Want from
Freelancing?, 12 / Summary, 17

2 What To Sell   19

What You Do Best, 20 / Other Marketable Skills, 23 / What
to Avoid, 23 / Sample Self-Analysis, 23 / Summary, 28

3 Finding the Business   29

Analyzing the Potential, 30 / Where to Look for Actual
Business, 32 / Where to Get Details, 35 / Summary, 38

4 Selling Yourself   39

Your Approach, 40 / Successful Follow-up, 44 / Competing
with Non-Freelance, 45 / Repeat Business and Referrals, 47 /
Freelance Security, 49 / Summary, 52

5 What To Charge   55

Deciding What to Charge, 56 / How to Apply Charges, 60 /
What is Chargeable, 67 / Summary, 70

6 Bookkeeping and Billing 71

Setting up Your Records, 72 / Billing Clients, 77 / Summary, 81

7 Money Matters 83

Freelance Budgeting, 84 / Equipment and Supplies, 89 / Government Requirements, 92 / Looking Out for Yourself, 94 / Summary, 95

8 Business Relationships 97

Ask Questions, 98 / Put it in Writing, 100 / Working with the Client, 102 / Staying Out of Trouble, 105 / Summary, 106

9 The Work Environment 109

Your Office Location, 110 / Maintaining the Integrity of Your Business, 114 / Summary, 115

10 Subcontracting for Services 117

Selecting Freelance Talent, 118 / Selecting Suppliers, 120 / Assuring Client Satisfaction, 120 / Summary, 112

Appendixes 123

A — Sample Cover Letter, 124 / B — Sample Summary of Services, 125 / C — Sample Personal Letter, 126 / D — Sample Bill, 126-27 / E — Sample Proposal, 127-28 / F — Sample Confirmation Letter, 129 / G — Sample Freelance Contract, 130

Index 131

Preface

This comprehensive guide to selling your freelance services brings together advice on many considerations of freelancers (or would-be freelancers) enroute to both personal and financial success. It is directed toward one-person, low-overhead, truly independent ventures offering any kind of freelance service. You may be just thinking about freelancing or already be at it; either way, you will find advice in this book helpful in making your decision about freelancing or in improving your business.

Many people consider freelancing the last, footloose resort when a "secure" job can't be found. Others think of it as a way to make money in a hurry. Freelancing can be several things, including vagabond and lucrative. It can also be so exciting and fulfilling that you'll wonder why you ever worked any other way. For you, it will be what you make it, which is why this book concentrates on how to look at yourself in relation to what freelancing is like and at your personal objectives for freelancing. It is not a get-rich-quick guide, nor a set of hard-and-fast rules, but rather a collection of advice based on experience that may help you decide about freelancing and/or be a success at it.

Because no two freelance businesses are exactly the same, your reactions to the guidelines presented here, plus additional words to the wise from your experience, will be appreciated. Please share them with me through the publisher so that we can pass them on.

I acknowledge with graditude the information provided by other freelancers, the advice of my colleagues in preparation of this guide, and the understanding which supports the way I like to work.

1 Is Freelancing for You?

"Ever want to get away from it all? Ever dream of a life of *adventure*?"

This introduction to an old radio drama may be a little extreme; but these or similar questions beckon people every day away from their eight-to-five jobs into a very different way of working — freelancing.

Some take the words literally and march blindly away from their employers, hang out a shingle and start freelancing. All too often, however, their visions of freedom and wealth turn into mirages as success eludes them. Feeling defeated, they go back to the eight-to-five, never knowing that, by thinking through what freelancing is like and planning for it, they might have succeeded — or decided in the first place that freelancing wasn't for them.

Several factors contribute to such disillusionment, but perhaps none as much as appreciating how freelancing corresponds with personal objectives, qualities, and desires. To help you focus on these considerations, this chapter first offers a common definition of what *freelance* is and examples of the types of freelancing people are actually doing. Then it discusses the objectives and drawbacks of freelancing, followed by a self-analysis exercise to help you decide whether or not freelancing is for you.

WHAT "FREELANCE" MEANS

Throughout this book, the word *freelance* is used to identify an independent person who provides services on a short-term basis to a series of customers, patrons, or clients. It appears in our language as one word or two (free lance), having originally described a knight or soldier for hire.

Freelance is used here synonymously with other labels such as *consultant* or *self-employed* which can refer to similar short-term, multiple-client situations. These other labels may sometimes have slightly different meanings; but for purposes of this book and the advice it offers, all of them are grouped under the umbrella of *freelance.*

What Freelancing Isn't

As stated earlier, a freelancer is fully independent—no employees, no partners, no incorporation papers, no or little inventory. Freelancing differs from other forms of business, even though a clear distinction isn't always immediately apparent.

Part-time is often confused with freelancing. They aren't the same, although they both occupy only a portion of a person's total work time. A part-time job pays a rate established by the employer for a task that needs to be done on a regular basis for fewer than eight hours a day. It may also include benefits such as medical insurance. A freelance project pays a fee established by the freelancer and agreed to by the client. The task is usually one that calls for special skills on a one-time or irregular basis. No benefits are included.

Some freelancers have part-time jobs to assure themselves of a stable income while they build up their freelance businesses. Others continue to combine the two because a sufficient volume of freelance work simply isn't available or because they don't want to break away entirely from the security of an employer.

An agency, firm, or other established small business also differs from freelance. The most distinctive difference is that such businesses need employees to support a volume of work that is more than one person can handle. With such size come the trappings of a formal business structure—payroll, substantial capital investments, inventory, office hours, and various set procedures. Structure and volume bring a certain predictability and security and may be your eventual goal: to grow enough as a freelancer to develop an agency or other business. If so, many books are available for specific advice on such a small business.

And Associates is a common business form that may be

the same as freelance, especially in editorial work. "John Doe and Associates" could mean that John Doe has an agency with employees. But more often it means that he has people on-call to provide skills related to his, as a given project requires. The name helps market full-service capability; but the form of business fits the definition of freelance.

What Can Be Sold as Freelance
People with professions, with vocations, with years of experience, and with none are today selling themselves as freelancers. For example, they may include the following titles:

Writers	Proofreaders
Interior designers	Space planners
Landscapers	Typists
Photographers	Models
Cabinetmakers	Radio-advertising producers
Paste-up artists	Political-campaign organizers
Crafts instructors	Program planners
Caterers	Wardrobe consultants
Wallpaperers	Picture framers
Carpenters	Housecleaners
Editors	Farm laborers
Special-event organizers	Graphic designers
Illustrators	Calligraphers
Marketing specialists	Artists
Tradeshow workers	Tailors

Any skill has the potential of being sold as freelance — provided enough people want to buy it, of course. In general, the most successful freelance ventures involve selling a skill, rather than a product, *per se*. Freelancing certainly results in a product (tangible or intangible), but one that is custom produced by selling a skill, rather than one that is pulled off the shelf.

Some skills, however, are more adaptable than others to freelancing because they don't require an organizational structure. For example, if you want to be a banker, you'll have to sell your skill to a bank. Or if you want to manage an accounting department, you can't do so as a freelancer.

Also, some skills are more financially feasible than others for a freelance business. For instance, tuning pianos can be a successful freelance business involving very low overhead and a portable skill that can be sold to as many (or as few) customers as you can find. Selling pianos probably would not, however, because of the need for a costly inventory, showroom, established hours, a delivery system, and maybe even employees.

Your chances for success increase in direct relationship to how talented you are at what you're selling—and at selling it. If you're a new graduate or someone switching fields, you *can* be a successful freelancer if you're able to learn quickly and convince clients of your ability. However, if you've been out in the business world for awhile and can take advantage of years of experience in a particular field, you'll be a big step ahead of the novice. Old-fashioned hustle has a lot to do with freelance success, too, for the new kid, as well as for the old pro.

WHY PEOPLE FREELANCE

What attracts one person to freelancing may differ markedly from what attracts another, just as to any job. Because the reason behind freelancing has a great influence on *how* you approach your business and even on *how long* you keep freelancing, a close look at what your objective or objectives really are is critical to your success. You might identify with one or more of the following common objectives.

Independence

At the top of the list for many freelancers is a desire for independence—an escape from the confines of an employer-employee situation. Freelancing allows you to set your own pace, accepting or refusing projects, working until a job is done, and taking off when you have nothing more to do.

You can schedule yourself, starting work at 4:00 A.M. or staying up until midnight, as you like. Such flexibility means you can work when you are at your best (rather than submit to the eight-to-five regimen) and get to the tennis courts or sale racks when most people are at the office or plant.

If independence is your objective (or one of them), make sure you are a successful freelancer because failure means giving up your independence for a traditional job. You will be committed to freelancing for the long haul. You can take on work that may go for months or even years with the same client, and your intention to stay in business can be used to sell that client in the first place.

Client relations will be doubly important. Be especially careful to satisfy so that you can count on future business. Burning bridges will destroy your enterprise and, thus, your independence. Also, you'll be continually marketing yourself so that the flow of business and income justifies your freelancing, instead of working for someone and earning more.

Income

Making money is an objective shared by every freelancer who isn't independently wealthy—which is just about all. Freelancing can be lucrative. If your business is well-managed and your fee in line with the market, you *will* make more than your full-time colleagues for the same hours worked, even minus the cost of your own insurance coverage and other overhead.

To improve your chances for making a lot of money, peg your business right in the beginning so that you're selling skills that have a market (see Chapter 2). Also, heed the advice throughout this book about finding projects, keeping records, and maintaining client relationships.

If your objective is to supplement another income, freelancing can also be your answer. For example, a retiree can freelance to earn extra dollars, as can someone working a full-time, but ill-paying, job. Look for the kind of assignments that will require only the time and energy you have available.

If your objective is to make enough money to finance a particular project (such as college expenses or an addition to the house), freelancing can, again, fill the bill. For short-term income, go for short-term work because, with this objective, your freelance business will probably exist only for as long as you need extra cash.

Variety

Some people want the constant change of projects and clients that can happen when freelancing, as opposed to the routine of a full-time position. Today's activities for the freelancer are unlike yesterday's or tomorrow's. Also, the clients are varied; even if you specialize in a particular industry, diversity exists in management styles and, of course, personalities.

Variety is a side benefit for some freelancers; they accept and enjoy it but don't seek it out. If it's a main objective for you, however, avoid settling in with a handful of clients who will take all your time indefinitely. You'll want short-term assignments so that the scene and cast of characters change frequently. You may also want long-term assignments as a secure base for your business; but you'll need to find enough other work that comes and goes to satisfy your thirst for variety. A mixture of assignments behind you can, in addition, help you sell future business because of such broad experience.

Respect

Another possible objective for you is getting respect for your skills. As an outside "expert," you will probably find that your advice carries more weight than identical advice from an employee. Indeed, some freelance assignments materialize for this very reason. The client has trouble winning over or satisfying the people upstairs. The solution: Bring in an outside expert to say the same thing to more receptive ears.

If respect is what you want from freelancing, you will need

to pay special attention to keeping up your quality and business image to support the expert label. You may even want to beef up your credentials with additional training.

Detachment

"In-and-out" is an objective of many freelancers who want to do projects but not get caught up in office politics or personalities. Any company, association, or individual has idiosyncrasies; if you would just as soon not find them (or succumb to them), freelancing can meet that need.

If detachment appeals to you, you will have to select assignments that have a definite beginning and ending (maybe that don't require you to go to planning meetings or make decisions) so that you just do the work and move on, keeping your investment in the organization or individual to a minimum.

Career Advancement

Freelancing can be an excellent avenue for career advancement. The assortment of assignments possible as a freelancer can be much greater than what a full-time employee is exposed to, and they can provide a continual opportunity for the freelancer to add and fine-tune skills.

If your objective is career advancement, you will want to find stepping-stone projects that lead toward improved qualifications as a freelancer or a competitive edge, should you ever want to apply for a full-time position.

Involvement

You may freelance as a way to keep active in your chosen field. If you've had to take a different type of job or to give up a position to be at home for personal reasons, you can use freelance assignments to maintain skills and contacts.

To stay involved, be prepared to put forth extra effort to freelance on the side. Develop a schedule and stick to it so freelance projects meet your needs without overwhelming your time and energy. Doing so may mean turning down clients; but special attention to client relationships (as discussed in Chapter 8) can encourage them to call again, rather than cross you off the list.

Survival

Your objective for freelancing might be economic survival. Many freelancers are simply filling the void with freelance projects while they look for full-time positions.

As a result, they must limit assignments to those that are short-term to avoid having to renege on client commitments when the freelance business is suddenly scuttled. If such a holding pattern is your situation, freelancing may even be your in to a full-time opportunity: By showing a client what you can do as a freelancer, you might be able to keep doing it as an employee.

THE DRAWBACKS OF FREELANCING

The coin, of course, has two sides. Freelancing has drawbacks which can strongly influence your decision to get in—or to stay. Qualities that are attractive to one person are insurmountable obstacles to another; among them are the following drawbacks.

Insecurity

At the top of the liability list for many people is the loss of security that is the tradeoff for freelance independence and variety. Insecurity has an influence on time, money, and emotions.

You will not always know what you will be doing tomorrow—or even this afternoon. As a freelancer, you can manage your own time; but you are also highly susceptible to client forces. They may not call until they're desperate and need your help *right now*. Or they may not call at all, after you've blocked out time for their work. Also, that two-hour project could be twice as large, and the onus is on you to do some fast shuffling of your schedule.

Income is not secure, either. A freelancer has to contend with whether or not work can be found and with when clients will get around to paying. Also, if you fail to negotiate well or run into complications with a client, you may have to sacrifice income to get out of a sticky situation with your reputation intact. "Feast-or-famine" is a common experience of freelancers, unlike the regular paydays of their full-time colleagues.

Time and income considerations aside, the insecurity that may have the greatest impact on you is an emotional one. Most of us are culturally geared to the eight-to-five and never think of living any other way. We've worked, slept, eaten, and relaxed for years around that routine so that the pragmatism of freelancing can be an unsettling jolt.

Don't underestimate the emotional influence of the uncertainty of freelancing on you and those close to you. Working erratic hours, worrying about finding your next project and weathering defeats and slow times will take their toll unless you learn to roll with them. You may have found a full-time job dull; but it was usually predictable. Freelancing isn't — at least for the majority of freelancers and certainly not for those just starting out.

Self-Responsibility

Hand-in-hand with freelance independence is also the weight of responsibility it brings — another quality that some people find a serious drawback to freelancing. *You* are responsible for you, and no supervisor or staff will bail you out. You have to market your service, stick your neck out to get and keep clients, meet every commitment, and be accountable for mistakes. As a freelancer, you have few places to hide and few clients who will shrug off poor scheduling or a less-than perfect product, as they might for an employee.

The marketing aspect alone is a heavy responsibility. The successful freelancer is not timid. You have to be able to talk about yourself, in writing and in person, to take being turned down time after time and still come back for more. If you don't like selling yourself or are unwilling to learn how to, either don't freelance or get an agent to take on that responsibility for a fee.

Intensity

Freelancing is a very intense way of working—more intense than full-time positions usually are. The successful freelancer puts forth full effort when the clock is running. Coffee breaks, chats with friends, long lunch hours, and other customary distractions of the workplace are not chargeable for the freelancer. You are paid for a particular skill and can expect to apply it in generous measure; so if you prefer a leisurely approach to working, you're probably not a prospect for freelancing as your primary income source.

Because of the intensity, five or six hours a day may be all you can work and feel as if you're giving your best. Your schedule and income expectations should be geared accordingly. Quite likely, you will never work so hard in your life, for prolonged periods, as you do when you're freelancing.

Detachment

The same detachment that appeals to some freelancers is a drawback for others. Your job is often implementation only—no helping to decide about scope, budget, or deadline. A freelancer many times isn't called in until those decisions are already made, and is then expected to abide by them. You will be paid to do what you consider mundane jobs or to clean up someone else's mess on an emergency basis because, as freelance, you are susceptible to anything the client will pay your fee to get done, even if it's not under the circumstances or of the quality you would prefer.

Don't expect to be showered with awards or to exercise great artistry or profound thinking; you may, but don't count on it. Your job is, to a great extent, to make your client look good upstairs. If your client wins praises for a project well done, you, in turn, will win repeat business. The client's objective for a given project must be yours if you are to succeed as a freelancer.

WHAT DO YOU WANT FROM FREELANCING?

Now that you know more about the pluses and minuses of freelancing, you must decide if it's really for you and, if so, what objective(s) you have. What appeals to you about freelancing? How important are certain drawbacks? Do you have what it takes to make it at freelancing as you now know it?

To help answer these questions, start with a review of the objectives and drawbacks, as just discussed. They were as follows:

Objectives	*Drawbacks*
Independence	Insecurity
Income	Self-responsibility
Variety	Intensity
Respect	Detachment
Detachment	
Career advancement	
Involvement	
Survival	

Now look at your own feelings toward these objectives and drawbacks, based on the following analysis of your qualities as a worker and person. Finally, put your evaluation into writing, in your own words, so that your assets and liabilities in relation to freelancing are clearly in mind, along with your objective(s).

Qualities of a Freelancer

As you can see from the list of objectives and drawbacks, your prospects for success as a freelancer depend on both capability and attitude. The following checklist is a guide to help you decide what those qualities are, whether you're only thinking about freelancing or rethinking your decision after being at it for awhile. Rate yourself one to five, then add up your score.

	Never			*Always*	
	1	2	3	4	5

Are You Competent?

Do you know what you're doing on the job?

Do you avoid getting in over your head?

Can you readily suggest a backup plan, when needed?

Can You Manage Yourself?

Can you make and stick to your own schedule and be efficient?

Can you manage money and expenses to make the most of limited resources?

Can you organize demands on you to meet old, as well as new, commitments?

	Never				Always
	1	2	3	4	5

Can You Sell Yourself?

Are you convincing in interviews? Can you handle them with ease and confidence? — — — — —

Can you be persuasive in writing? — — — — —

Are You Self-Motivated?

Can you come up with fresh ideas for doing your job? — — — — —

Can you bounce back after a defeat? — — — — —

Are you a self-starter? Can you set a schedule and prod yourself to meet it? — — — — —

Can You Analyze Yourself?

Can you see where you might improve certain skills? — — — — —

Do you know when you have done well or poorly? — — — — —

Can You Accept Responsibility?

Do you make firm commitments and follow through? — — — — —

Do you admit mistakes? — — — — —

Do you look out for your own interests? — — — — —

	Never 1	2	3	4	*Always* 5

Are You Flexible?

Can you put forth extra effort when work demand is high and find something to do when demand is low? — — — — —

Can you work for today and not worry about what you have to do tomorrow? — — — — —

Subtotal — — — — —

Total ——

If you're not sure how to answer some of the questions, ask your spouse, friends, and/or associates to give you their impressions. A total score of only sixty or less indicates a lack of qualities that can make you a successful and happy freelancer. A higher score with only a few points off throughout the checklist is a reasonable base for continuing your plans to freelance. However, several points off in one category is not. Freelancing requires a variety of qualities; one or two long suits won't do it.

What's In It for You?

Now, take your reactions to the objectives and drawbacks of freelancing and your responses to the checklist and convert them into pros and cons of freelancing for *you*. From this summary, come up with as definitive a statement as you can in answer to the question, "Is freelancing for you?" Following is an example.

Pros	*Cons*
I would like the independence of freelancing versus a regular job.	I've never worked on my own and don't know how well I would do.
I like the idea of having variety in my work.	
I can have much-needed time at home to get things done and still earn money.	
I might make more money freelancing than working for someone.	I may not initially — or ever.
I know what I'm doing and where to go for help when I get stuck.	
I've always managed time and money well to make both stretch.	I'm not sure about the uncertainty of freelancing. I've always had a regular paycheck and steady work.
I'm not rattled by job interviews and talking about myself.	
I know when I've done well and when I haven't.	I don't like being turned down or defeated and take awhile to recover.
I've always felt responsible for myself; no one looks out for me better than I do.	
I get along with a mixture of people.	

Is freelancing for me? It is if I can find enough work to fill my time and make enough money to offset the insecurities. My objective, then, is to freelance so that I can be independent and enjoy variety in what I do. I would like to freelance indefinitely but, for the short-term, my objective is to get experience marketing myself to see if it's really feasible.

If this self-analysis has been encouraging, read later chapters for details about selling yourself, money matters, and other considerations of freelancing, then return to this exercise to see if your thinking has changed. If you decide to freelance, you will probably find that the objective(s) you set now won't be exactly the same as you will have later. Your degree of success, full-time job offers that are enticing, and personal factors are some of the continual influences on how long and why you freelance.

If, on the other hand, the cons outweigh the pros, reconsider your plans to freelance. Many would-be freelancers let the desire for independence and perceived high income override reason — and soon find themselves having to swallow their pride and admit they made a poor move.

SUMMARY

- *Freelance* refers to someone working independently to provide a service on a short-term basis to a series of clients.
- Freelancing is fully independent (not an agency, firm, or other established business) and differs from part-time in how a project is priced and length of involvement with a client.
- *And Associates* is frequently used by a freelancer to sell the full-service capability of having other skills on-call.
- The most successful freelancers sell skills, rather than products, per se.
- Skills that don't convert well to freelancing are those that require the structure of an organization, or those that have high overhead.
- Your chances for freelance success are better if you have experience, but the beginner can succeed by learning quickly and marketing effectively.
- Objectives of freelancing include independence, income, variety, respect, detachment, career advancement, involvement, and survival.

- Drawbacks of freelancing include insecurity, self-responsibility, intensity and detachment.
- Qualities that increase chances for freelance success include competence, ability to manage and sell yourself, self-motivation, ability to analyze yourself and accept responsibility, and flexibility.
- When listed as pros and cons, your strong points should clearly overwhelm your weak points if you expect to succeed as a freelancer.

2 What To Sell

If you have decided that you have the qualities suitable for free-lancing, the desire to give it a try, and your objective(s) in mind, your next step is to determine what service or services you will sell. The choice might appear obvious: "I will sell myself as a residential landscaper." Or, "I will do fund-raising."

Be aware that a quick and simple statement is not a solid foundation for your business because it may overlook skills that could produce income, or be an emotional, rather than rational, choice. This chapter takes you beyond the obvious, breaking down the question of what to sell into component considerations. You'll put them back together in the end to see what might be your primary freelance service and secondary offerings, as well as what you should avoid to keep your business on track.

WHAT YOU DO BEST

The logical place to start in deciding what you will sell is with what you have the most of, and do the best. Training, experience, psychological factors, and how others evaluate your work are all parts of this multi-faceted decision.

Following are questions to help you think about these areas. Add to or modify the list to correspond with your particular situation and jot down your answers. Then ask yourself what you should sell, based on your responses. At the end of this chapter is an example of how answers to this section and the two that follow might look, including an over-all summary statement.

Training

Skills in which you were trained, either in school or through workshops or conferences, should be considered.

1. What was your major in school (high school, trade school, or college)?

2. What was your minor?
3. Do you have a diploma? Degree(s)?
4. Are you licensed, certified, or accredited?
5. Have you had additional training, such as special classes?
6. Do you go to professional meetings, read trade magazines, or in other ways keep up with what's new in your field?

Experience

Especially if you are many years beyond school, your experience will tell you more than your academic record about what you can now sell successfully. To answer the following questions, look at what you have actually gained from experience, both on the job and off.

1. Do you have a solid foundation of experience in your chosen field?
2. Have you had progressively more intense and responsible positions?
3. Has your experience had a common core, even though you may have had different jobs?
4. What do you consider your strongest qualifications for your present (or immediate-past) job?
5. Have outside experiences contributed to your skills? How?
6. What three things learned from experience have helped you the most to be where you are today?

Successes and Failures

Training and experience must be tempered with other considerations to select your most marketable skills which are reflected in your success record.

1. Do you feel that, in general, you have been successful in your work?
2. What have been your greatest successes so far?
3. What have been your greatest failures or shortcomings?

Enjoyment

Another factor influencing your decision is how much you have enjoyed doing whatever you have done because, unless you enjoy freelancing, you won't make a go of it.

1. Do you like working in your chosen field?
2. What have you enjoyed most about the jobs you've had? Outside activities?
3. What parts haven't you enjoyed?

Level of Involvement

What you sell is also influenced by the extent you want to be involved in projects — in other words, whether you want to provide yourself can save you hard and costly lessons later.

1. In the past, how involved have you been in your work? Were you mostly a thinker or a doer?
2. What amount of involvement has given you the greatest satisfaction?
3. What amount would you like to have?

How Others See You

Your decision will benefit from a look at how others see your skills. You can answer these questions yourself; but to get a complete picture, discuss them with associates.

1. What comments have been consistently high in job evaluations?
2. What improvements have been suggested?
3. What do your associates think are your strongest skills?
4. Your weakest?

Based on answers to these questions, summarize what you could and would want to sell right now as a freelancer, then go on to the following section.

OTHER MARKETABLE SKILLS

Next, look at other skills that might help your chances for success on the freelance market. They could be either secondary skills related to your primary one or weak skills that, with a little effort, could be developed and sold as part of a package.

1. What other skills do you have related to your main one(s)?
2. Could any of them be sold now or developed?
3. Can you strengthen weak skills so they could be marketed?

Into a simple statement summarize what you might sell as secondary skills and/or what you could develop to sell, then complete the following section.

WHAT TO AVOID

The other consideration that's part of your analysis is what to avoid in your freelance business. What you already know about yourself can save you hard and costly lessons later on.

1. Under what conditions have you done poorly?
2. What have you done that you have thoroughly disliked?
3. With what kinds of people and/or organizations have you not enjoyed working?

Draft a simple summary of this section, also.

SAMPLE SELF-ANALYSIS

Following is an example of how such a total self-evaluation might look, and how summary statements from the sections add up to an over-all statement about what your freelance business could offer.

Training

1. What was your major in school (high school, trade school, or college)?
   English literature and education
2. What was your minor?
   Library science
3. Do you have a diploma? Degree(s)?
   B.A.; working on M.B.A.
4. Are you licensed, certified, or accredited?
   No; but I plan to become an accredited business communicator
5. Have you had additional training, such as special classes?
   Workshops and seminars on photography, writing, interviewing, tape/slide shows and correspondent networks
6. Do you go to professional meetings, read trade magazines, or in other ways keep up on what's new in your field?
   Yes

Experience

1. Do you have a solid foundation of experience in your chosen field?
   Not really; I wouldn't say it's solid
2. Have you had progressively more intense and responsible positions?
   Yes
3. Has your experience had a common core, even though you may have had different jobs?
   A common core exists in my job pattern; each job had increasing difficulty and involved communication skills
4. What do you consider your strongest qualifications for your present (or immediate-past) job?
   Learning fast
   Understanding what needs to be done and doing it
   Writing skills
5. Have outside activities contributed to your experience? How?
   No; my experience is all on-the-job

6. What three things learned from experience have helped you the most to be where you are today?
   Being treated poorly in some jobs, showing me what I don't want to do for the rest of my life
   Like to work with people and am good at it
   To let people know when I've done a good job

Successes and Failures

1. Do you feel that, in general, you have been successful in your work?
   Yes
2. What have been your greatest successes so far, including job and outside activities?
   Producing well-written and designed materials
   Involving people in their newsletter
   Succeeding in a communication job with no formal journalism training
3. What have been your greatest failures or shortcomings?
   Need more experience with management
   Need to be more assertive

Enjoyment

1. Do you like working in your chosen field?
   Yes
2. What have you enjoyed most about the jobs you've had? Outside activities?
   Variety
   Feeling of creating something worthwhile with my skills
   Interaction with people
   Opportunity to learn
3. What parts haven't you enjoyed?
   Having managers who don't know what they're talking about and won't admit it
   Not being able to control schedules, yet being accountable for finished products
   Not being able to take time off or vacations when I want
   Politics of organizations

Level of Involvement

1. In the past, how involved have you been in the work you did? Were you mostly a thinker or a doer?

    Both. Responsible from concept through finished product

2. What amount has given you the greatest satisfaction?

    Everything but production details

3. What amount would you like to have?

    Would like to give someone else responsiblity for production phase of projects

How Others See You

1. What comments have been consistently high in job evaluations?

    Good writing skills

    Enthusiasm

    Always go above and beyond

2. What improvements have been suggested?

    Writing of employee benefits; need more work

    Being more assertive

3. What do your associates think are your strongest skills?

    Ability to work and plan independently

    Learning quickly

    Liking challenges

4. Your weakest?

    Not well enough rounded in experience; no audiovisual work

Summary: I am competent to sell myself as a communicator for mid-level development and writing assignments that offer variety, self-direction, and the ability to control schedules, without having to handle production details.

Other Marketable Skills

1. What other skills do you have related to your main one(s)?

    Photography; technical writing; possibly training (education degree)

2. Could any of them be sold now or developed?
   Yes
3. Can you strengthen weak skills so they could be marketed?
   Improve audiovisual skills with classes and seminars; possibly use library-science minor to get experience as research assistant

Summary: I could use photography and technical-writing skills now and possibly improve skills in audiovisual and research.

What To Avoid

1. Under what conditions have you done poorly?
   When I have too many projects at once so that I can't devote my attention to each one
2. What have you done that you have thoroughly disliked?
   Working with people who plan unrealistically
   Being a secretary and a typist
3. With what kinds of people and/or organizations have you not enjoyed working?
   People who change their minds all the time and still expect me to stick to the schedule
   People who don't respect my abilities and want me to prove myself constantly
   Jobs or companies that offer no freedom to try new things

Summary: I should work for people who make and stick to decisions in an environment of mutual respect and freedom to experiment.

Statement of What To Sell

I could freelance as a writer and as a planner for corporate-communication programs that are small in scope. I could also freelance as a technical writer or research assistant. I want to work with managers who are intelligent and in positions to get things done, in an environment where my abilities are recognized and respected and where I can control schedules without having to handle production details.

SUMMARY

- Analyze training, experience, successes and failures, enjoyment, level of involvement, and how others see you to decide what you might sell as your primary freelance service.
- Consider other marketable skills that could be secondary freelance services.
- Look at your likes and dislikes to see what to avoid in your freelance business.
- Summarize your findings into a clear statement about what to sell as a freelancer, what could be developed, and what work or situations to shy away from to increase your chances for success.

3 Finding the Business

Although you're not a "big corporation," you want your freelance business to be as successful as one. Therefore, you'll need to do as they do in the beginning and throughout your freelance career: Know your market.

This chapter can help you do just that, starting with how to gauge the amount of business that may be out there for you. The section on where to look offers suggestions about ways to find particular projects; then the chapter concludes with recommendations for tools to assist in your research into specific prospects.

Such market analysis is an investment of your time against an eventual return you hope is not *too* eventual. How much time you invest in this analysis depends on how well organized you are, what channels of information are already open to you and how accurately you can predict your chances for success.

Obviously, you can't keep looking forever; at some point you'll have to be realistic in the face of no business, cut your losses, and look for alternatives to freelancing. If you're freelancing for short-term income only, that point may be soon so that if nothing turns up, you can look elsewhere without having lost much time. However, if freelancing for you is to be a long-term venture, be prepared to invest weeks or months checking out the market and prospects before your business is up and running. And expect to spend many hours writing letters, calling, and pounding the pavement, not once but continually to replace and add clients.

ANALYZING THE POTENTIAL

If you can, start feeling out market potential while you still have a full-time position so you can make progress toward a successful freelance business at the same time you are enjoying a regular paycheck. However, if circumstances force you out into the cold before you've been able to collect any or much information—or if after an easy start, your freelance business has bogged down—

get to this analysis right away so you can regroup as soon as possible. If you're a beginner, think through market potential before you spend money for an office and equipment to assure yourself that you're making a wise investment. People who can help you test the market are suggested as follows.

Associates

Your business associates (co-workers, colleagues, suppliers, and others actively in business) can be gold mines of information from their different perspectives on the market. Ask them if they see room in the market for the freelance service you propose to offer or if they see that your fledgling business has room to grow.

If they know your work well, ask them for an honest appraisal of how it stands up against similar work they've seen in the open market. They don't have to judge its quality against an ideal, but rather against what others are providing. Your work must be at least as good as what is already available to clients in the marketplace — and certainly can be better.

Buyers of Freelance Services

Ask people you know who buy freelance services how they see the market. If they say calls come every day from freelancers looking for business in your field, they are telling you that the market is saturated. Either rethink your decision about freelancing, or develop a variation on your service or a more productive and creative approach to prospective clients that will set you apart from your competition.

Associates may be able to refer you to buyers of freelance services whom you don't presently know. With someone to introduce you and help you get appointments, you can talk informally, without pressing for any business. How do they see the market for your service? How do they react to various approaches (as discussed in the following chapter)? What are they currently paying for your kind of service?

Other Freelancers

If you know other freelancers or can get introduced to some, you can glean valuable information from this source. Find other freelancers by asking your associates and people you know who buy freelance services. Contact trade and professional associations locally (or nationally if local groups don't exist) for names of other freelancers in your area with a similar skill to offer. When you find one, be sure to ask if that person knows others. Keep a list of phone numbers since freelancers can help one another by sharing business, as well as advice.

If a freelancer offering a similar service will even talk with you, you have a clue that the market has room for at least one more. If the person won't talk or gives elusive answers, be forewarned that, at least in that freelancer's eyes, the market isn't large enough for another entrant.

Ask other freelancers about their projects and how many hours of work they average per day or week. If the climate is conducive, get into specifics about approaches to clients that have been effective for them and about going rates (see Chapter 5). Translate their answers into your own objectives for freelancing. For example, if a freelancer out for supplemental income has aggressively looked for business but found only enough work to meet that limited objective, can you expect to find enough to support yourself entirely, month in and month out?

WHERE TO LOOK FOR ACTUAL BUSINESS

Assuming your research indicates a high potential for freelance business of the type you plan to offer or presently do offer, you will next need to consider where to look for clients (or new clients). The sources will certainly depend on what you're selling; but following are some common possibilities which you can try, in addition to others your research so far may have unearthed.

Former Employers

If you have left former employers on a positive note, check with them for possible work. They are familiar with your skills, although they may need to be updated to understand how those skills have increased or improved. Follow up with a summary of your service (see Chapter 4) and send a business card — or several — to encourage them to make referrals for you.

Suppliers

You may be the first to know of business opportunities if you maintain contact with suppliers of related services. These people get into offices all over town and can tell you not only who's doing what but how well (a point to remember when you need to check a prospective client's reliability). Ask them how often they hear of a need for your skill and request that they keep you in mind when they do. Refresh these contacts from time to time to underscore that you're really interested in hearing from them. If certain suppliers don't know you well, give them a summary of your service and several business cards for referrals.

Established Businesses

The task of marketing yourself won't be as large if you can find established businesses to sell in your behalf. For example, if you are offering a freelance service related to interior design (such as paperhanging or specialty woodworking), contact interior designers. From their positions with furniture stores, corporations, or their own businesses, they may get clients with several needs (among them, your skill) and subcontract with you to be able fully to serve those clients.

But you have to find the established businesses that can use you. Look for them through suppliers, other contacts, and the Yellow Pages. You may have to write many letters and make many phone calls. However, the payoff can be great in terms of busi-

ness for you and time saved by not having to market yourself
directly and continually to individual prospects.

Other Freelancers

Just as they can help you analyze the market, other freelancers
can help you find business. Keep in touch with those you know
or to whom you've been introduced. Make sure they are aware
of what service you offer. Successful freelancers often have more
work than they can accept and, if they know you're competent
and interested, may send some your way.

Also, freelancers providing services related to yours sometimes need collaborators to help them offer a comprehensive package to clients. For example, an architect will call on a variety of
related skills before a project is completed. Make certain other
freelancers know you and your work, and encourage a mutual-
aid arrangement.

Unfilled Vacancies

Another place to look for business is with organizations which no
longer have someone on staff providing your service. An employee's leaving doesn't necessarily mean that the work has been
fully absorbed into another position. Usually something falls
through the cracks (especially an activity that is done infrequently), and it may be a project that just fits your freelance
capabilities.

Even in a situation in which someone has been promoted to
fill the vacancy, you may be able to get some business by offering to work with the less-experienced person on unfamiliar projects. Find out about such situations by talking with your various
contacts and attending trade or professional meetings where such
news is spread.

Listing Services

If you are a member of a trade or professional association, determine if its local chapter has an active listing service. Such a service
is usually open to members only and free to those listed and to

those looking for people. Call the person in charge and explain the kind of work in which you're interested. Ask what sort of freelance jobs are listed and with what frequency, then find out how you can participate. You will probably need to send your resumé or a summary of your service so that the listing person has your qualifications and phone number at hand.

At least initially, ask to hear about *any* freelance project available to ensure that you will do the screening, instead of the listing person. After you have worked together for awhile (and you are keeping busy), you can afford to let the listing service be more selective.

To maintain your good standing, always let the person know when you hear of a job or when you have more work than you can handle alone. Such volunteer listing services will be more receptive to you when you treat them as two-way streets.

The Want Ads

Although somewhat of a long shot, the classified section of your newspaper may give you business leads. Certainly check the part-time category (which is probably where the paper puts freelance listings). But also keep an eye on full-time positions in your interest area that have been running for weeks because, if employers are having trouble filling them, they might be talked into getting the work done on a freelance basis.

If you do respond to such an ad, clearly indicate that you are offering to make a proposal to fill the need as a freelancer, not as an employee. Such situations require a lot of convincing to shift thinking away from full-time. Quality for the dollars available is often the persuasive factor.

WHERE TO GET DETAILS

Research into the market may net possibilities but not enough information to approach a prospective client comfortably aware of that client's business and need. You will have to dig deeper

with the help of tools available to your trade or profession and
to the general public.

Directories

For specific names and addresses of organizations or individuals
possibly worth contacting, consult trade and professional association directories. They are usually listed by both name and subject
categories. For example, Allied Steel would be under "A," as well
as "Steel" or "Fabricators." National directories may be of some
help, although current local ones will probably be more so. If you
don't have copies as a benefit of membership, borrow from someone you know or consult a public or university library.

If your target audience consists of manufacturers, retailers,
and other "commercial" concerns, check with your local Chamber
of Commerce in the United States, Board of Trade in Canada, or
its equivalent. Such an organization may have current directories
for sale or gratis that provide considerable information, including
sales volume, number of employees, specific products, and chief
executive officers. Inspect library copies before you decide to buy
your own because they can be expensive. Assume a margin for
error in data that is solicited only once a year for such directories
and verify it if you can, especially names and titles of company
officials.

Financial Information

Another place to look for details or at least a flavor of a company
is in its annual report. A local, publicly held corporation may
have an annual report on file in your public or university library;
otherwise, call or write for one. If it's a subsidiary without its own
report, ask for the parent company's report which should include
specific comment about the subsidiary.

Read quarterly reports of public corporations and other financial analyses you can find, as well as your library's file of newspaper and magazine clippings on the organization. If need be,

ask your local newspaper or other publication to see what it has on file in its library.

The Yellow Pages

Don't overlook the Yellow Pages of your phone book. You may glean information from a company's listing and display ad about scope of operations, territory, and even sophistication as indicated by the quality of the ad. Also, an ad may give you useful technical words unique to that industry or company — language which you can use in your approach to the company as an edge over any competitors for that freelance business.

Contacts

No amount of library work can substitute for knowing someone close to the organization who can give you insight into its people and operation. Tap friends and associates who may know something or who can help you track down details. Especially if that contact is an employee of your target company, do not ask for proprietary information such as plans for new sales campaigns. Stick to who's who, position in the industry, growth potential, and other general questions that give you useful information, without compromising your source.

The Switchboard

When you have all the information you can get and are ready to make your approach, call the organization's switchboard to confirm spelling of the name and the correct title of the person you are about to contact. ("I'm addressing some correspondence and need to confirm if Pat Smith is still president . . .") You should *never* rely on names taken from professional directories or other sources — they may not be current. If you have no name, simply ask who's in charge of the department or type of project you have in mind. All your research will get you nowhere if you make an obvious mistake at this point.

Maintaining Useful Files

Organize the information you find so you will have everything in one place for easy reference. Use a card system or comparable method that will work for you. Clip together all your notes, supplemental material about a prospect (such as an annual report), and any correspondence.

Also keep a file on contacts, especially on other freelancers and their services. One source may be more familiar with a certain industry. Another may be somewhat unreliable so that you must always verify the information received. Make notes on all such details to fine-tune your market-data machine.

SUMMARY

- Analyze potential business by making use of information from associates, buyers of freelance services, and other freelancers.
- Use former employers, suppliers, established businesses, other freelancers, unfilled vacancies, listing services, and the want ads as sources for business leads.
- Tools that will assist your research into particular prospects include directories, financial information, the Yellow Pages, and various contacts.
- Maintain a comprehensive file on all prospects, as well as on your contacts.

4 Selling Yourself

The next step toward a successful freelance venture is to decide *how* you will get the business you have decided is out there. This chapter discusses various approaches to making your service known and securing projects, as well as how to compete with non-freelance. A section on repeat and referral business presents suggestions about how to take full advantage of such windfalls, followed by how to plan and organize for freelance security.

This chapter presents general tips on freelance selling. For detailed information on the fine points of selling yourself, consult the many books published on that specific subject.

YOUR APPROACH

After you've found prospective clients, you must approach them in such a way that you walk out with a project or leave them informed and impressed enough to call you for future work. Your approach will depend somewhat on the service you are offering; however, following are some universal suggestions.

Word of Mouth

Nothing communicates quite as effectively as the grapevine, and you should make constant use of it. Assuming your work is worthy of praise, the loudest and most productive voice singing your virtues will be that of a satisfied client. Word-of-mouth recommendations can also come from colleagues, suppliers, and other contacts familiar with your service. Even a chance encounter at a party between a former client and someone who needs your service can give you an entrée.

Feed the grapevine every time you have reason to be in touch with one of your contacts. Mention a current project, a new area into which you've recently expanded or similar comment that will refresh or update information contacts have about your service. Let them know that you're aggressively looking for new business by saying so.

Of course, word of mouth can as easily work against you if your performance has been poor. Be careful whom you ask to speak in your behalf. A dissatisfied client obviously won't be your first choice, nor a client with whom you've had a difficult time, regardless of the outcome of the project.

Summary of Service

If you don't have someone who will take you in hand to a prospective client, you will have to make your approach in writing. You could make the initial inquiry by phone or in person; but you will be courting failure by doing so, especially if you're looking for corporate clients. People seldom appreciate the interruption of someone's calling or walking in and trying to give a full-scale sales pitch. Therefore, your time will, in most cases, be better spent first putting that pitch into writing.

One of the simplest ways is to summarize what you offer, the experience that backs up your ability to provide that service, your training, and any other statements that might help sell for you, such as a general or specific list of recent projects. Such a summary of service is an informative piece to enclose with a cover letter. Use the letter to highlight particular interests or skills from the summary that are especially relevant to the recipient.

Your summary differs from a resumé in two respects. One, it consolidates the information usually included on a resumé into a capability format that presents the essential points in prose, rather than outline, leaving out extraneous matter. Two, it looks different from the usual experience/education resumé which is associated with a job application, thus helping avoid confusion that you might be after permanent work.

Depending on what is appropriate for the service you offer, your summary can be simply typed and photocopied on white paper, and your cover letter typed on quality bond. Typesetting and printing your summary and putting your cover letter on a letterhead may be preferred if you are selling yourself to an executive audience or if you are, say, a graphic designer and want the approach itself to advertise your talent. One advantage (besides cost) of typing your summary is that you have the option of tailoring your material to a given prospect and, thereby, making your pitch more individual. Such a personalized approach can also indicate that you are very interested in the prospect and not just sending a standard form.

Do not, however, discard your resumé. Once you've opened discussion with a prospective client, you can use your resumé to give specifics on qualifications, work history, education, and other details which may be required. Clients who aren't accustomed to buying freelance are especially oriented to resumés and may not make a decision about using you until they see this customary verification of credentials. For an example of a cover leter and summary of service, see Appendices A and B, respectively.

Printed Brochure

Instead of a summary and cover letter, you might opt for a brochure that substitutes for both or for just the summary. A printed brochure may be your choice

- when a high level of sophistication is expected by your audience for the service you offer, for example, if you conduct training seminars for corporate executives.
- when you want to lend a note of stability to your freelance business, for example, if you're a bookkeeper competing with established firms.
- when a mass mailing is your marketing approach, for instance, if you are a wedding photographer.

Your brochure should read and look at least as polished as anything your competition puts out. The fact that it's printed requires all the information to be relevant to each recipient. Any time the brochure might be directed toward a specific prospect, it could be accompanied by a cover letter personalizing the information. Your fee could be printed in the brochure; but if you expect to change it, make a general reference to your fee in the brochure ("I work either by the hour or by the project . . ."), then give a specific figure in your cover letter or in a separate price sheet.

In addition to outlining what service you offer, the brochure should summarize your qualifications in a paragraph or two and might also include your photograph or other artwork appropriate to your business. If you're spending the time and money to do a brochure, get the advice of a graphic designer if you aren't skilled in that area. As a low-overhead substitute, find a format you like and work with your printer to duplicate it. Consider making it a self-mailer to save the cost of using envelopes or designing it so it can be posted on bulletin boards if you might expect calls from such exposure.

Your brochure need not be extravagant in design, art, and paper but should be flawlessly typeset, printed and folded, and present well-written copy and quality artwork. Remember that it will represent you until you have the chance to do so yourself.

Personal Letter

This approach has limited application since, in the format of a business letter, you can't present a lot of information. But it may be your choice if you are approaching someone whom you know quite well and who is already acquainted with your work — or someone to whom you can write, using the name of a close associate as reference.

Opt for a personal letter when you are virtually certain of getting an interview or referral but want to be more formal than a phone call. State your availability and desire to talk — but first be certain that the acquaintanceship on which you're basing your use of this approach is solid and not a passing business or social tie.

For an example of a personal letter, see Appendix C.

SUCCESSFUL FOLLOW-UP

Whether you use one of the written approaches suggested or another you think particularly effective, you must follow up in a way that will give you the best chance for a personal interview with a prospective client. Short of presenting yourself on that prospect's doorstep, however, you have no guarantee that you will get close to an interview, unless the mention of a mutual friend obligates the person to hear you out.

Probably the most common method when you have directed your inquiry to a specific person is to indicate in your letter that you will follow up by phone. If you are approaching a private individual, someone in a small company, or a middle manager in a large organization, state that you will follow up your inquiry directly to that person during a certain week or after a certain date. Usually one to two weeks after the letter should have been received is sufficient; if you wait longer, the person may not remember you. Avoid giving a specific day or hour, unless you are absolutely sure you can make the call then. Build in some flexibility so you're not pressing or jeopardizing your reliability by missing your own deadline.

If you're writing to a busy executive, consider asking in your letter if you should speak with someone else ("I realize you are very busy; so if you would prefer that I talk with someone else . . .") Also state that, unless you hear otherwise, you will call to follow up. If you are not contacted in the meantime with the name of another person in the organization, call the executive's secretary. Give your name, the date of the letter, and its subject. An efficient secretary will know to put you through to the executive, ask you to leave a message, refer you to someone else in the organization, or say they're not interested in your service.

Consider enclosing a return postcard if you are doing a mass mailing, and if you think an executive will most likely pass your information on to a subordinate. The card could be returned immediately to request more information or an interview, or be kept for a later date when your service might be more timely to the organization. Such a card can be filled out with little effort and give you a feel of client interest, without the time investment of phone calls.

Your objective by phone or return postcard is to explain you service in detail, in person, or at least, through additional correspondence. You may not get it and should not make a pest of yourself trying. If the best response you can elicit is, "We'll keep you on file," you are at least ahead of where you started.

Keep a complete record of each approach and its outcome if you are put off or turned down. A reminder months later may have a more encouraging reception from a client who has to "ripen." Also, renew your contact if the unresponsive person moves on; the replacement may be of a different mind toward what you have to offer.

COMPETING WITH NON-FREELANCE

Your service may be one that competes head-to-head with a full-time employee or an established business. In such circumstances, you will have to sell yourself as the better choice. To do so, consider when a prospective client most likely would turn to outside talent.

When Time Is Short

Freelancers can frequently come to the rescue in an overload situation. Time is short for employees; but the deadline must be met. As a freelancer, you can take the pressure off, either by doing the overload project or by relieving an employee to do so by temporarily taking over regular duties.

A client will, obviously, have to spend some time to find and interview freelancers, select one to do the job, and give full details about the assignment. But the few hours invested to bring in a freelancer will take less of the client's time than would doing the project itself. A client will be even more likely to call you in if you have done your marketing homework and already have information about your service on file so all the client has to do is pull it out.

When Skill Is Short
You can also come to the rescue when in-house talent is not available for a special project. Employees may take care of day-to-day work, but not have the skill necessary when an odd job comes along.

A freelancer accustomed to doing that kind of project has the specific skill to produce a quality product and do so efficiently. The client, then, gets the job done without adding an employee who can't be justified in the long run or without assigning an unskilled person and jeopardizing the outcome.

When Money Is Short
As a freelancer, you might compete with an established business in either of the above circumstances, but may find that you have an edge when a shortage of funds is also part of the equation. For example, an engineering firm could go to a temporary-service agency for a typist to do a large report — or to a freelance typist. Quality and efficiency aside, the cost difference could be substantial. With the first option, the client will have to pay the agency *and* the typist. With the second, only the typist is involved, and the bill will probably be less because of lower overhead costs for the freelancer.

You will still have to contend with what some clients feel is the prestige of an established business, its impression of permanence, or the ease of dealing with one business for multiple needs versus with multiple freelancers. However, use your ability to do quality work, your scheduling flexibility that comes with independence, the personal attention you can give to a project, and your low-overhead operation against these arguments. They can win you the business against stiff competition.

REPEAT BUSINESS AND REFERRALS

To save yourself the time and energy required to ferret out and get business from new clients, use every project to encourage a windfall of repeat and referral business. The more work you can do for a client and the more you can get that client to sell for you, the more time and energy you will have left over to put into projects, rather than promotion—and the more successful you will be.

Doing Your Best

Probably the simplest way to be considered for repeat business is to do the best possible job on a client's initial project. If you know the client could have a lot of work for you, bend over backwards (without giving away your time, of course). Going the second mile may win you an excursion ticket—an exclusive on all that client's business.

Quality performance time after time will also be rewarded by referrals. As mentioned earlier, the grapevine can be a potent marketing tool. Nurture it by doing a first-rate job so the client will speak highly of you to others.

Asking for the Business

Don't be afraid to make your bid for repeat business in person and in writing. When you turn over a completed project, reach for the next one ("I enjoyed working with you and look forward to being involved on your next project . . .") When you send your bill, include a similar comment. If the client has mentioned a specific, future project, don't hesitate to recall it ("Please let me know when the park project is ready to go . . .").

Also don't hesitate to ask for referrals: "I hope you've liked my work and will recommend me to your friends . . ." The quality of your work should speak for itself; but a gentle nudge won't hurt. If the client is receptive, leave behind a few business cards to back up those referrals.

Keeping in Touch

The fact that you have completed your assignment and received your check should not close the door on a client relationship. If you think similar projects will come up from time to time, keep in touch with the client to underscore the fact that you're still around.

Renewing contact by phone is one method if your target isn't a busy executive. Have some reason for the call, other than "I just called to chat." Clients usually have other things to do. For example, look for items in the paper or comment on something you see the client has done ("I noticed that you've been promoted . . ." or "I saw the latest magazine and want to say what a great job . . .")

If you think the client would not appreciate the disruption, keep in touch through samples of your work. If your freelance service results in tangible products (such as printed material, technical reports, or drawings), share copies with past clients and include a personal note explaining what the piece is and indicating you are available, should the client again need your service.

You can even schedule ahead if your service is needed on a regular basis, such as preparing tax returns. When you've completed this year's, set a time to meet with that person to start on next year's, then call a month ahead to confirm. Such long-range scheduling may be too regimented for your freelance spirit — but if not, it does assure you of repeat business.

Responding to Clients

A sure way to lose clients is to ignore them when they contact you. Responding in a timely fashion to phone calls and letters may seem elementary, but is so often overlooked as a basic mark of your reliability as a businessperson.

Even if you are too busy for more work or don't want to be involved again with a difficult client, return a call anyway. Courteously decline the business and refer the person to someone else, if you can. No response says you're not interested — which may be true today but not in a few months when business is slow.

Maintaining and Expanding Skills

You will have more repeat and referral business if you keep up the level of your skills and expand them. A start-up project may lead directly to an offer of a more complex (and profitable) one. Be prepared to accept it with confidence.

One way to do so is to take on paying or volunteer projects to gain particular experience or sharpen rusty skills. For example, if your talent is sewing custom-made clothing, do the costumes for a community theater to broaden your skills and business base. Whether the work is for love or money, you still benefit from the experience.

Another way to keep up with your trade or profession is through reading, attending meetings and conferences in your field, and taking classes to expand your horizons. Such investments of time pay off in other ways, too, most especially in keeping up your contacts.

FREELANCE SECURITY

Your initial goal as a freelancer will be to sell yourself with enough success to *get* into business. However, the first time you experience a dry spell of some duration, you will quickly start thinking about how you can develop sufficient freelance security to *stay* in business.

As stated earlier, freelancing doesn't have the security of a regular paycheck. Many people think it can't even come close; but with attention to how and where you market yourself, it may. As a matter of fact, freelancing can, in a sense, give you a more secure feeling because *you* are in control, even if business is slow. As a freelancer, you will never go to work one day and discover your "secure" job is gone. You may lose clients; but if you plan ahead, you won't lose your entire income when you do.

Analyzing Your Mix

Start with taking a close look at the kind of assignments you have had. Depending on your business, you may have had a wide variety or projects that are similar. But each has surely been different in some way, if only in the personalities involved. Thus, your mix of work and clients can influence your security as a freelancer.

If you find yourself stretching yourself to the point at which you take a project (even if you don't feel qualified, have the time, or work well with the client involved) and do it poorly, limit your scope for *effectiveness*. Your objective must be satisfied clients who will give you the security of calling again and amiable relationships that won't leave you frazzled and unable to perform well on your next assignment.

If you find yourself driving all over town or otherwise incurring high overhead costs, limit your scope for *efficiency*. Similarly, poor scheduling that results in large gaps during the day for which you aren't paid is lost income.

Another consideration that can lead to greater freelance security is how much predictability you have in your client mix. For example, if your work has consisted of one-time projects only, look at cultivating at least a few clients who are predictable in both time and income. A commitment of twenty hours a month at a guaranteed fee to a particular client can be a comfortable security blanket. Also comforting is the assurance that a client will always call you first when your kind of project comes along.

After you've been freelancing for a few months, you'll develop a feel of how much predictability you need for emotional well-being. If you're biting your nails from anxiety about tomorrow, to the detriment of your work today, build in more predictability for peace of mind. All your business need not be regular; you'll have to seek your own level of emotional security. Some freelancers can handle four different projects and clients a day; others want only one or two.

Decisions that result from a look at your mix have obvious financial implications. You may be able, for instance, to cut overhead costs and/or to average more working hours in your day by scheduling your time better or limiting the geographic area in which you accept assignments.

Also, you can more easily increase your rate with one-time or sporadic clients than you can with regular ones. Your fee for a regular client will remain the same as when you started or increase infrequently; the tradeoff is a consistent fee for consistent work. Irregular clients, on the other hand, see you once or seldom; with them, your fee can more readily increase as you think experience and skills justify charging more.

To meet your income expectations, decide what percentage of your time should be devoted to regular versus irregular clients. For example, a mix of two-thirds predictable and one-third not provides income stability, but also a sizable portion that can readily be charged an increased fee.

Knowing that you can expect so much per month from predictable work also helps cash flow. You can budget according to the minimum that will come in and know you'll be covered.

Weathering Slow Times

The other aspect of freelance security is how to keep financially and emotionally stable when business is slow, despite your best efforts. The time of year, economy, and probably other factors indigenous to your service will have a very real influence and may be more than all your selling skills can counteract. So, what can you do when you have nothing to do?

Make sure you have a cash reserve to tide you over and eliminate immediate concern about how to pay your bills. You'll have to gauge according to your own experience; but figure you could use at least three-months' worth of savings as a comfortable reserve.

Also, make sure you have a project reserve to keep you active and mentally up. Clients with rainy-day projects on the shelf would be ideal. But they're not common; so you will more likely need to come up with your own.

If you could use a vacation or time to catch up on work around the house, take advantage of the break and do so. If, however, you need to feel you're putting your freelance skills to some use, volunteer your time to keep active, write a professional article, or contribute your service to a friend — whatever fits your skills and interests. Of course, avoid overcommiting yourself because, when the phone finally does ring, you need to be able to drop what you're doing and make some money.

Set yourself a mental minimum of effort you'll put forth each day or week to generate business and a maximum of how long you can reasonably hang on to hope that your service will sell again. As in any other business, don't get in unless you are prepared to accept that influences beyond your control can force you out. For example, some freelance services are especially susceptible to economic factors that you can't control (such as design or photography which aren't purchased when money is tight). Other services (such as home repair or fiction writing) have a more steady market. If yours is a volatile service, accept the possibility that, someday, the market may force you to decide if staying on your own is realistic. After you've weathered a slow time or two, you'll discover how much security, both financial and emotional, you really have and need.

SUMMARY

- Approaches to prospective clients include word of mouth, a summary of service with cover letter, a printed brochure, and a personal letter.

- Don't make your approach until you know how you will follow up; most likely, it will be by phone.
- Gear your sales pitch around the fact that clients consider freelance when they are short of time, in-house talent, and/or funds; also emphasize your scheduling flexibility, specific skill, and low overhead when competing with non-freelance.
- Cultivate repeat and referral business by doing your best on all work, asking for the business, keeping in touch with clients, responding promptly to client inquiries, and maintaining and expanding existing skills.
- Build freelance security by analyzing your mix for effectiveness and efficiency, including financial and emotional predictability.
- Weather slow times with a cash and project reserve and set a minimum you will do each day or week to find new business and a maximum amount of time you can afford to wait for work to materialize.

5 What To Charge

You're talking with a prospective client and have explained your service, qualifications, and, perhaps, how you would do a particular project. Then comes the question, "What do you charge?"

This chapter helps you come up with an answer that will be competitive, as well as sufficient. It covers how to determine what and when to charge, what activities and expenses are chargeable, and methods of applying charges.

While this advice is directed primarily toward the beginning freelancer, it also has application if you've been on your own for awhile but haven't earned as much as you had hoped because your fee scares away clients. Or you want to raise your fee but are afraid of losing your clientele. Attention to fee is a continual part of freelancing, whether you're a newcomer or an old hand.

DECIDING WHAT TO CHARGE

The decision about what to charge for your service obviously influences how much money you make. Undercharging means you will put in many hours just to meet your minimum income expectations. Overcharging means clients will go elsewhere for lower-cost services. Either way, you won't make much.

Also, your fee is a statement of what you consider yourself worth, as is the pay attached to any job. However, as a freelancer, you — instead of an employer — are putting a price tag on yourself. What that price tag is says a lot about *you*.

In buying freelance, a client is buying specific, "expert" talent to help out on a short-term (often crisis) basis, with no obligation to provide you with an office, vacation, training, or the other amenities of full-time status. The marketplace allows you to take these factors into account when you quote a fee. Therefore, your fee will be higher than what an employee is paid — but so are your particular skills, risk, and personal responsibility for your work.

While you will probably adjust your fee as you improve

your skills and gain more experience, you'll want to try to start out neither too high nor too low. With either extreme, your business could fold for lack of income and/or clients. A little time applied in the beginning to research can help you make a wise selection.

Salary Surveys

One source of data for your research is salary surveys for your field and geographic area. While most such research applies to full-time positions, it can be useful in helping you narrow down the question of your market value. For example, if a survey shows that the average annual salary of someone with your skills, experience, and education in your part of the country is $20,000, you will know that to make full use of your talents, you should shoot for at least that much (plus the value of employer-paid benefits) as a freelancer. Otherwise, from a purely marketing standpoint, you should sell your services to a full-time employer and make more without all the risks of freelancing.

Salary surveys can also indicate trends to give you an idea of how your fee might change over the years and in relation to new skills, more experience, and additional training. If you're making $20,000 now, a survey may tell you what your earnings as a freelancer should be in five years to keep pace with your peers. Always figure in the value of benefits; bonuses also come with some upper-level jobs. That $20,000 position could be worth $25,000 or more, all things considered.

Many associations regularly do salary surveys, as do active local chapters of such groups. Check with them and, even if all you can find is a national survey, look for data broken down by region. Another resource is your public library, as well as colege, university, or vocational-school departments that provide training in your field. Ask what research has been done recently. Also, check with your local Chamber of Commerce, Board of Trade or its equivalent, and large financial institutions with published market research that might have bearing on your particular service.

Other Freelancers

Pair the indirect approach of surveys with a second, more direct source of information about fees: other freelancers. As stated earlier, if you don't know any, get names from your contacts and people who buy freelance services or check with trade or professional groups. Even if you find only one or two, you will probably get useful information.

Your inquiries may have to be cautious, especially if you don't know the freelancers well enough to ask what they now charge.

- Determine if the person is selling a comparable service. ("What sort of projects have you been doing?")
- Get an idea of the person's competence. ("Have you been in business long? Do you have clients who call on you again and again?")
- Find out what experience the person had prior to freelancing. ("What were you doing before you started your own business?")
- Determine what the person charged in the beginning. ("May I ask what your fee was when you started out?")

You may get a wealth of other information, especially if the market is open and the person isn't threatened by your entering it. However, if you are able to ask only the kind of questions outlined, you will know what a given service, provided by a person with a certain background and qualifications, was worth at a particular time. Then you can compare that situation with yours for a better idea of the current value of your service in the marketplace.

Another method of checking what other freelancers charge is to ask the people who coordinate listing services. As mentioned in Chapter 3, you'll want to know them, and they can give you at least a range of what others who are listed are charging.

Buyers

A third group to research is people who frequently buy freelance services. Discuss rates as you talk with them about the market in general, as also advised in Chapter 3. Don't assume that, because you may later approach someone with an offer of your services, you cannot ask questions now. Buyers interested in the best quality for their money always like to know who is available. If you convince them of your abilities, you will probably find them very willing to help you get off to a successful start.

If your freelance service is writing (or related), consult your library's current edition of *The Writer's Market*. It offers an indirect look at what buyers of editorial services are paying. Evaluate the fee range for your skill according to your level of experience and what your local research had indicated as acceptable.

Established Businesses

A fourth gauge to use in determining your fee is what established businesses are charging for the same service. For example, if you're selling writing skills to corporations, ask someone who uses or works for a public-relations agency what the current hourly rate is. Or ask related suppliers such as printers or typesetters. This rate is the one clients are now paying; so if you can match the quality of service, you can charge a similar rate. However, be sure what the agency rate includes — for example, if some expenses (such as photocopying) are part of the package. Will you charge extra for those? If not, your fee must cover them, also.

Consider setting your fee lower than that of an established business to give yourself a competitive edge. You will run into clients who question whether or not your service is really comparable — or, as mentioned in the last chapter, who simply prefer doing business with someone who obviously has stability, plenty of backup support, and an impressive list of clients. You may not be able to counter all these points; but at least you can offer a budget advantage.

HOW TO APPLY CHARGES

Almost as disparate as methods of charging are ways to apply those charges. Most likely, you will either work on an hourly basis until the project is done or estimate the time required and be paid by the project. Other possibilities are working on speculation and on retainer. You'll also need to decide if you will charge a consistent or variable fee and when and how to raise your rate.

Hourly Rate

A strictly hourly rate has advantages for both you and the client — and disadvantages. By charging in direct relationship to time spent, you are paid for exactly what you put into a project. If the client changes the requirements or otherwise frustrates completion of the work, you are covered for any additional expenditure of time. The client enjoys a similar protection against an overcharge by you for more hours than were actually worked, assuming the client has an idea of how much time might reasonably be involved.

A drawback for you with an hourly rate is that a job could take less time than you had guessed; had you bid it, you would have made more than your hourly rate. A drawback for the client is that a freelancer could pad out a job, taking advantage of the client's inexperience or rush situation.

Charge by the hour when

- requirements of the job are unclear and susceptible to change;
- you're working with a new client and want to protect yourself against an unknown;

- the client wants a strict accounting of hours and won't accept a bid;
- you don't want to take a chance on bidding too high and losing future business or too low and losing money.

Bids and Estimates

In certain circumstances, a package cost will be preferred and even required by one or both parties. Those situations might include the following:

- Requirements of the job are clear and will not change along the way, and both sides want predictability of time and cost.
- The client and freelancer have worked together before and understand one another so that the project should proceed smoothly for the time estimated.
- The client must budget a set figure for the work.
- The freelancer expects problems and wants a guaranteed (and high) return to compensate.
- The client suspects the freelancer won't make the most efficient use of time and wants to avoid spending more money than is available.

A firm *bid* is a commitment to do a given job for a given fee. You may put more or less time in than you thought; but your bill is for the agreed-to figure.

An *estimate* gives the client a probable cost, based on your understanding of the work required. It differs from the bid in that both sides recognize that it isn't firm. If you work fewer hours than you estimate, you will bill less. Conversely, if you work more, you will bill accordingly.

The advantage of the bid is that you can, conceivably, make more — if you're skilled at predicting, if you can limit your time and still turn out a quality product, and if the work doesn't drag on and on, eating up your profit. You can also lose your shirt from unanticipated overruns. The more frequent occurrence is the latter.

The advantage of the estimate is that both you and the client have flexibility, should the project be larger or smaller than originally thought. From your estimate, the client can budget close to the eventual bill. Also, any efficiencies you can effect to reduce charges below estimate will help keep you in good standing with the client.

This second method can also include a built-in stop—a stipulation that the client will be warned if the work threatens to go beyond the estimated figure. Then a decision can be made about proceeding. This kind of fair dealing pays off in your being able to finish what you've started and in repeat business from a satisfied client.

If you're a beginner, work on an hourly basis whenever possible until you build up enough experience to make knowledgeable bids or estimates. You may encounter some jobs that require a firm bid, and from them, you'll learn quickly how to estimate because you'll probably make costly misjudgments.

Out of increased experience will come records that can be invaluable in helping you bid and estimate jobs. For example, if you're selling a housecleaning service, keep track of how much time is required to do certain tasks in given situations. By reviewing your records and adding together the components that apply, you can make a close estimate for a new job of the time required to clean a three-bedroom, two-bath home for a family of five.

After a point, you may no longer need such detailed records. However, unless you do exactly the same thing for each client, don't give up your record-keeping. Especially if your bid or estimate for each new job must account for ever-increasing supply costs, make sure you know what those costs have been.

Speculation

Looking at a project on speculation may be required if you are competing with another freelancer or an established business for a major job. For example, a company might want to change the interior walls in its building and will decide, on the basis of competing feasibility statements, who will do the whole remodeling project. As a freelancer, you are asked to be among the architects competing.

The disadvantage of spending time on such speculation is, of course, that you will have exerted effort with no guaranteed return. You will simply have invested your time in hopes of a payoff.

Before getting involved in a speculation situation, make sure you have protected yourself. Understand enough about the project that you are convinced you can do it, that you can make money, that you have a chance against competitors and that the client is firmly committed to proceeding with the work.

Then put forth only as much effort on speculation as is necessary to start the clock on a pay basis. In the example, inspect the building and do some sketches. Do not spend hours on detailed drawings. You won't stay in business if you throw away all your time on speculation. While you can't prevent a client from giving your ideas to someone else to execute, you can protect yourself beyond the idea stage.

A client may respond favorably to your plan and ask you to prove your worth by completing a part of the work. Advance with caution if you choose to advance at all. Get the client to agree that, should you be selected to do the work, you can charge retroactively for the portion already done.

Retainers

Another way of working is on retainer, a form applied to an arrangement whereby a client has someone on-call whenever a particular service is needed. A maximum number of hours per month may be set with an hourly fee beyond that ceiling, or a lump sum paid for whatever the volume of work happens to be.

A retainer can be a security blanket for both you and your client, providing you a guaranteed income and the client a predictable service. Similar to working for a flat fee to complete a given project, you will need a retainer sufficient to cover the hours you will spend, on an average, if you're paid a lump sum per month. You may also consider a higher retainer than your per-hour rate would otherwise be to compensate for always being available to a client and, because of that fact, having to turn away other work.

Because you may want the retainer raised over time and because you may need the data to estimate other jobs, keep track of your hours, if not the exact activities performed. For example, if you are retained to do bookkeeping for a small company and have based your asking price on an average of twenty hours per month, you will be losing money if your records show you are actually working thirty.

In the case of a full-time retainer to perform a given long-term task, gauge your asking price against what you could be making on a purely freelance basis on the open market. Also, consider what the job would be worth if the client were to hire an employee to do it.

Consistent vs. Variable Fee

Once you set your rate, whether by the hour or by the project (based on your estimate of hours required), decide if you will charge it consistently, regardless of the assignment. In other words, if your rate is figured on $40 per hour for photography, will you charge the same for darkroom time? And what will you charge for any clerical time involved in a project?

Freelancers differ in their answers to these questions. One school holds that time is time. If you weren't doing the clerical portion of a project, you would be free to take on more work. Thus, the rate should be the same.

Another school holds that the emphasis should be on the value of the type of work performed. Because on the open market clerical activities are valued down the scale, the fee for that portion of a project should be less.

Your choice about which way to go rests, to a great extent, on your appraisal of just how successful you are. A freelancer in demand can more easily command a consistent rate than can one who is grateful for whatever comes along. Also, some clients will require a fee difference while others will not raise the point. State your fee and say it applies to all work on a project, if that is your choice. Then, if the client doesn't bring up a fee break, don't volunteer one. However, if the client does, talk about it long enough to sense how strong that position is, then decide how badly you want the work and how important maintaining the client relationship is. Whether you charge full fee or compromise, be sure that your agreement is spelled out in writing to the client, in advance of the start of work (see Chapter 8).

Raising Your Fee

The rate you set today most probably won't be what you would like to charge a year from now. Assuming you get better at what you do and in greater demand, the market says you can justify a higher fee. You will need to keep pace, especially if your business is susceptible to increasing supply costs.

Some freelancers don't raise rates, feeling that the service provided today is the same that was provided three years ago and, therefore, should cost the same. If your skills have remained constant, if your costs haven't gone up, and if you are happy with your income, then don't raise your rates. The chances are, however, that at least one of these factors will change so that you'll want to consider raising your fee.

If, on the other hand, you think your rate is too *high* and find that business isn't coming your way as a consequence, coming down is easy. When you talk with prospective clients, quote your lower rate.

Raising your rate with new clients is relatively simple, also. State your charge as your *current* fee. By using the word *current*, you are leaving the door open for a possible increase at a later date. Also, you are covered should a new client confer with an old one you have listed as a reference and find a discrepancy in fee.

A tougher environment in which to raise your fee is one in which you feel at home. Repeat clients may be your mainstay and, if so, they represent a major portion of both your income and your job security. Thus, you run the risk of serious ramifications if your approach about a higher rate backfires.

A client with business maturity realizes that increased competence and service longevity warrant an increased value on that service, just as employees earn merit and annual pay raises. If you are working with someone to whom such a statement would probably be a surprise, think twice about trying to adjust your rate. If you value the business, you may decide to leave well enough alone. Or you could lessen the room for argument by proposing to raise your fee a comparable percentage to what the client's employees received for the year.

If your service is in demand and you know you can replace any business lost because of the price tag, go for what you want. Then, if a longstanding client falls by the wayside, you can fill that time more profitably with someone new, billed at a higher rate.

To make your fee requirement known, talk with the client face-to-face, if you can. Out-of-town clients will probably have to be handled by phone or mail. Be prepared to substantiate your claim to more money — and prepared to back off or terminate the relationship if the client doesn't see your worth as you do.

In conjunction with that discussion, put the fee change in writing. Indicate your rate increase and its effective date on the next bill to the client or write a separate notice and send it to the client immediately after you have come to terms.

Also, consider producing a small announcement to be mailed to all clients if you have several and wish to institute a blanket increase. It's a method many suppliers use to let everyone know at once of the increase and, because of its form, to indicate that no client is getting preferential treatment. It isn't a substitute for direct discussions with frequent clients, but can be used with infrequent ones.

WHAT IS CHARGEABLE

Once your fee is determined, you and your clients will have to agree on what is chargeable. Although clients can certainly object (and, on rare occasions, even be generous in your direction), the decision about *what* is chargeable is as much yours as is the decision about *how much* to charge.

Time

As a freelancer, you charge for actual time devoted to a project, on behalf of a client. One of your strongest selling points is that you charge only for the time spent (unlike the cost of maintaining a full-time employee, regardless of the amount of work that really gets done).

Beyond this general statement, time charges depend on individual situations. The time you spend conferring, drawing up a proposal, and presenting it to the client is chargeable if you and the client agree that it is. Otherwise, it isn't; the clock starts when your proposal is accepted. (See the previous "Speculation" section in this chapter.) Clearly state at the time (and back it up in your written agreement) when you will start work.

Exceptions are an arrangement in which the freelancer is on-call to provide a given service or in which you are told, "We want you to do the project. Come in and we'll get started." The clock starts running when the work is initiated. This point should be made clear to the client at the onset.

Always discuss the financial arrangement before you get into the work. Then you will avoid putting in time, only to discover the client had a different understanding. Many people don't

like to talk about money; successful freelancers aren't among
them.

Expenses

Another point on which you'll have to settle with clients is the
charging of expense items. As a guideline, anything purchased especially for a particular project is chargeable to that project.
Anything purchased to enable you to provide your service is
your overhead.

For example, a freelance caterer for small meetings and
parties can charge a client for food and any special items bought
for the event. Not chargeable are the china, silverware, and linens
needed to allow the caterer to provide the service. Those things
must be covered by the fee as overhead.

Some freelancers apply a markup to supplies purchased for
a client to compensate for the trouble of doing so. An alternative
is to charge for the time, exact cost of the items, and any mileage
needed to get them. Choose one or the other, but not both; don't
charge time, mileage, *and* an inflated price. Your intention should
be to make money on your service, not on expenses, and clients
will appreciate such fairness.

Travel

Freelance practices related to travel vary widely. The options
include

- charging mileage and time for local travel needed to execute
  a project, but not to get to and from the client's office;
- charging portal-to-portal mileage and time, regardless of the
  reason for the trip;
- charging either mileage or time for the above, but not both;
- charging full fee for out-of-town travel for an assignment,
  plus transportation and related expenses;
- charging a partial fee (often one-half) for such travel time,
  plus expenses, with the actual work at full fee;

- charging a per-day or half-day fee for out-of-town assignments, higher than your regular per-day or half-day fee for in-town work to compensate for the extra overhead and travel time.

Your choice among these or other options depends on what is customary in your type of freelance business (other freelancers and frequent buyers can tell you) and on how successful you are. If demand is low, be prepared to compromise. Just make sure you and the client agree on how travel will be charged.

What you charge for mileage is your determination. Some clients, however, won't pay more than they pay their own employees. If you charge at least as much as you can deduct for tax purposes, you will be dealing fairly. If a client won't pay the equivalent rate to what you can deduct, record the difference to declare on your tax return as uncompensated mileage required to conduct your business.

Meetings and Mistakes

The question sometimes arises about charging for meeting time with the client to talk about a project after work has started. Such time is definitely chargeable. To do a project well, you need input from the client as you go along. It's a legitimate requirement and, thus, a legitimate charge.

If, however, the client calls a meeting to evaluate your progress, with the obvious implication that someone is dissatisfied, sacrifice your time to save the project. You are responsible for the quality of your work and for your efficiency in performing it. The client should not be expected to compensate for your shortcomings.

A related problem can occur if a project or portion of one must be redone because of an error on your part. Assume the time to do so is on you unless the client offers your full fee or a percentage of it. Also, be prepared to assume responsibility for other costs related to the project, such as reprinting a brochure because of your mistake. Knowing your financial liability can be so major, make a habit of thoroughly clearing work with the client *before* getting to the expensive stage. The following chapter contains details about recording time and expenses for client billing and future reference.

SUMMARY

- Research salary surveys, other freelancers, buyers, and established businesses similar to yours to decide what to charge.
- Apply charges by the hour or according to a bid or estimate for the whole project, depending on the situation.
- Do as little work as possible on speculation before turning it into a pay project.
- Even when working on retainer, keep track of your time to avoid sacrificing income for security.
- Apply your fee consistently to all work if you're successful enough to have the opinion that time is time; vary your fee by project complexity if you're not, or if a client requires that you do.
- Raise your fee cautiously to protect old client relationships, and always communicate the new fee in writing.
- Charges for time, expenses, travel, conferences with clients, and the cost of mistakes depend on agreements with clients, as well as local and acceptable practices.

6 Bookkeeping and Billing

Important considerations on the money side of your freelance business (in addition to fee) are bookkeeping requirements and billing procedures. This chapter provides advice on setting up accurate and efficient records, where to go for accounting help, what to consider when billing, and how to handle supplier charges and clients who delay or ignore paying you for your work.

SETTING UP YOUR RECORDS

As stated in the previous chapter, keep accurate and detailed records to account for time and expenses. That information should be sufficient to tell you

- charges to date on a given project;
- total time and expense charges by project and month;
- time requirements for portions of jobs (for reference when estimating new projects);
- how much of a payment is for services versus expenses;
- billing and payment dates;
- total income for the year;
- deductions as the cost of doing business (overhead).

If your previous work experience has been in salaried positions, you will find this much bookkeeping quite extensive. Once it becomes routine and you see how it can keep your business running smoothly, however, you'll realize that keeping records takes less time than *not* keeping them.

Documenting Time and Expenses

Your biggest aid to maintaining order will be entering information as you have it. When you finish working on a project for the day, record your time. To aid your memory when work is varied, note as the day progresses how you allocated your time. When you have mileage or other expense charges, write them down. Enter a supply purchase the day you make it.

Another aid will be a well-stocked stationer for bookkeeping forms. They are available in a variety of formats, and you may have to look at or try out several before you find the one that best fits your service. Some are hardbound books, others tablets, and still others loose pages in binders, all of varying sizes. The loose-leaf format gives you flexibility in how your records are organized and allows you to use any leftover pages another year. The size depends on your filing system and the amount of freelance and expense activity you expect to have.

Specifically, the information a ledger form should accommodate includes the following:

- Name, address, and phone number of the client
- Rate charged
- Date work was done or expense incurred
- Activity performed and for how long
- Charge for activity or expense
- Total charge for services
- Total charge for expenses
- Date of billing (and second billing, when necessary)
- Date of payment
- Date, type, and amount of deductible expenses for your business

You may not find a standard form that will take care of all your needs; but you can modify or even develop your own and photocopy it. Following is a sample of how information might be entered. Be sure you can read your writing days or months after the fact and use a pencil for easy correction of bookkeeping errors.

Record charges for time and expenses separately so you can have a clear picture of actual income as you go along. Also, computing income at tax time will be quicker if you don't have to split out expenses. Following is an example.

ADDRESS <u>1743 Jackson Ave.</u>   CLIENT <u>Dependable Finance</u>

<u>Harper, LA 49362</u>   RATE <u>$20/hr.</u> SHEET NO. <u> 3 </u>

DATE	ITEM	PER UNIT	DEBIT	CREDIT
7-14	Article: Research	2.50 hrs.	$50.00	
7-16	Article: Interviews	2.00	40.00	
7-17	Article: Writing	3.25	65.00	
7-17	Photocopies	—	1.10	
7-20	Article: Rewriting	.75	15.00	
7-21	Billing for services	—	170.00	
7-21	Billing for expenses	—	1.10	
8-15	Payment for services	—	—	170.00
8-15	Payment for expenses	—	—	1.10

The same form used for deductible items would appear as follows.

ADDRESS <u>   </u>   CLIENT <u>Office Expenses</u>

<u>   </u>   RATE <u>   </u> SHEET NO. <u>   </u>

DATE	ITEM	PER UNIT	DEBIT	CREDIT
7-1	5% Mortgage		$32.50	
7-4	5% Utilities		4.24	
7-4	Extension Phone		2.10	
7-28	Typewriter Repair		23.70	

Each client or category of deductions should have its own page or pages, depending on volume. The grouping of deductions will depend on what service you're selling and business expenses. For example, your categories may include transportation, office, supplies, postage, and miscellaneous.

Receipts

Any item deducted as overhead should be substantiated by a receipt. Develop the essential habit of asking for receipts. File them as you make purchases for your business or pay bills (noting what they're for), then organize them at the end of the year for tax reference. Set up a long-range file to keep them for several years (ask your accountant how long is necessary), as you should other business records.

Receipts for items for which you will be reimbursed by a client should be filed separately. Simply clip them to the client's page in your ledger so you won't forget to attach them to your bill when the project is completed. Or set up a "Client Expenses" file that you go through at billing time.

Accounting Advice

To get you started on the right foot with your records and to help you anticipate tax requirements, seek reputable accounting advice. The United States Small Business Administration, the Department of Industry, Trade and Commerce in Canada, or its local equivalent can provide such counseling at little or no cost.

If, however, you expect to need help each year with taxes and occasional advice throughout the year, an accountant is probably your better source. The difference in cost may well be justified by the continuity of service you will receive and the time you'll save not trying to ferret out information yourself from a variety of tax forms, government brochures, and accounting books.

Your accountant can play a strong supporting role in your business; so select with care. Look for someone who is firmly established, accessible when you call, and interested in your venture. Not every accountant fits these qualifications, especially the latter. Your accountant should take your freelance business as seriously as any other. Also, be wary of using your cousin or next-door neighbor because the price is low. You'll be more apt to get the service you need when the relationship is business only.

If you have a personal accountant already, stay where you are for your business, unless that person doesn't want to be involved. With increasing reliance on computers to figure such things as equipment depreciation, continuity of all your tax records can avoid mistakes, confusion, and possible expense if a new accountant charges extra to duplicate your computer file.

If you don't have an accountant now, ask your banker, a respected business owner in your community, or a successful freelancer to recommend someone. Another source is the nearest chapter of the Society of Certified Public Accountants or a similar professional association in your area. Try to avoid picking a name out of the phone book and, for convenience, look for someone close to your office.

If you haven't yet started your freelance business, talk with your accountant now and ask about records and taxes to help you get going. If you've been freelancing for a few weeks or months, take in your records to make sure they're sufficient — and check that your information is correct about what is tax-deductible as a business expense.

Make sure you can call whenever other questions arise and ask how the accountant bills. The practice may be to charge for only the time required to do your return, even though you have questions periodically throughout the year. Or you may be charged a consulting fee for advice, as well as a fee for doing your return.

BILLING CLIENTS

Once you've set up your books and are in business, you will, of course, want to start billing clients. After all, that's the only way you'll get paid. Read the following suggestions, then check with your accountant if you feel you need additional advice.

Project vs. Month

Your billing will most likely be either by the project or by the month. Project billing is used when you have a clearly defined job and do not expect to be continually busy with work from that client. Monthly billing is used when separate projects are not so well-defined and when work is continuous.

For example, if as a space planner, you reorganize the executive area of a company's headquarters, bill for that project when it's completed to the client's satisfaction. If you are asked to meet all the space-planning needs as they arise, and one overlaps another or you do them simultaneously, bill by the month. Once you understand a new client's requirements for your service, recommend one method or another and ask to switch if circumstances change.

To help cash flow, your objective should be to bill as soon as possible after a project is completed. If you have been doing work for a client for some time and billing by the month but see nothing else coming up for several weeks, ask if you can bill immediately upon completion of the current project, whenever that is.

Likewise, if an extensive project is expected to last for weeks or even months, negotiate billing in stages to give yourself some income and to protect your time investment along the way from any payment delay in the end. For example, you may want to bill after the planning stage, then after the execution and evaluation. Or if the job is to last for six weeks, bill at the midpoint and end.

Monthly billing need not be exactly at the end of the month, as long as the client is aware that you schedule differently. If you must pay your bills at the first of the month, consider billing clients on the fifteenth or twentieth or every two weeks to help your cash flow. If, for example, you produce a monthly magazine that's delivered on the tenth, bill immediately afterwards. Bill consistently; don't send your statement early one month because you need the money and late the next because you didn't get around to making it out.

Client Requirements

At the same time you agree on when to bill, find out what the client requires from you and how soon payment can be expected after billing. One client may want an invoice for each project as it is completed, then a monthly statement. Another may simply want a detailed statement. Don't hesitate to ask since misunderstandings about billing can be as hazardous to client relations as misunderstandings about projects.

Especially in large organizations, accounting procedures may be streamlined for bills below a certain amount and more complex and time-consuming above that figure. So if you send two small bills rather than one large one, you may be paid faster. If the client suggests this type of billing, include a comprehensive statement for the files to avoid confusion about the total charge.

Ask if a signed bill typed on your letterhead or plain white paper is satisfactory or if you should use the kind of form available at a stationer's. You can certainly have special forms printed; but doing so will probably be unnecessary overhead. Also, ask to whom the bills should be directed. Is one copy sufficient? (*Always* keep a copy for yourself.) Can you expect payment within two weeks? Thirty days?

Client requirements for what appears on your bill also vary. A simple form is a summary noting your charges for a given project, plus any expense items. This method can be used when primarily one task is performed, for example, conducting an affirmative-action workshop for supervisory personnel.

More complex is an itemized statement detailing all activities by date and time. For instance, if the workshop was only part of a package that included a brochure and revisions to a supervisory handbook, all activities would be itemized. See Appendix D for a sample of an itemized statement.

Some clients prefer a combination of the two — a summary which can be sent to the accounting department for payment and an itemized list that can be filed for reference. The method used depends on your service and clients. Discuss this aspect with each client to avoid any complications — especially a delay in payment caused by a billing method that wasn't compatible with a client's accounting system.

Supplier Charges

Another decision you and the client may need to make concerns how supplier charges will be billed. For example, if you provide a freelance landscaping service, will you buy the shrubbery, sod, and other materials and add that amount to your bill, or will the nursery bill your client directly?

The decision has a definite impact on your cash flow. If *you* pay suppliers, you will be out that money until the client pays your bill, which could be weeks if the project is a long one. If suppliers bill your *client*, they control when they ask for payment. Your concern should be for fair, timely business dealings with both the clients and your suppliers.

Unless suppliers or the client objects, ask that invoices be sent to your attention from the suppliers as charges are incurred so you can verify their accuracy. Then hand them over immediately to the client for payment. If supplier charges haven't been paid from those invoices, ask suppliers to send monthly statements directly to the client.

This way, you have responsibly approved all expenditures

on behalf of the client, yet kept your personal funds out of the transaction. And suppliers will be paid as fast as (if not faster than) they would be if you weren't involved since you've been feeding the client invoices as they've come in, instead of waiting for the monthly statement.

If a supplier wants payment immediately and will deal only with you, not the client, try to put charges on a credit card. For example, if you fly somewhere for a client and must pay for the ticket yourself when you pick it up, use a credit card. By the time you get the bill from the airline, you'll probably already have the reimbursement from the client. Again, keep your money out of client/supplier transactions, whenever possible. Otherwise, you'll find yourself extending the client credit.

Past-Due Bills

Standard business procedure is to expect payment within thirty days after the date of a statement. Your bill is past due, then, if you have waited a month for a check and none has arrived. Discuss with a new client *in advance* what follow-up is preferred because, even in the best of businesses, delays occur, and neither you nor the client wants to jeopardize your relationship because of a clerical error or misunderstanding.

The most efficient — and usually sufficient — course of action is to call the client and say that you are about to send a bill for recent work and need to know if you should note the unpaid balance. Or if you're not doing more work for that client, simply report that you haven't received payment and ask when you might. You will probably get an apology and an immediate check since reputable businesses (like individuals) don't want to have their tardiness pointed out.

The next step if payment doesn't arrive is to do a second billing, either by reference on a new statement as above or by sending a copy of the delinquent bill with a note indicating it is past due.

If such phone calls and statements bear no fruit after sixty days, ask yourself if you were clear about what schedule of payment was expected. Was the client really satisfied with the product? How valuable is the client to your business versus the size of the bill?

One option is to reiterate your bill and say you will not accept any more work from that client until it is paid. Another is to add finance charges to your second or third notice (generally 10 to 20 percent of the unpaid balance). And obviously another option is to drop the whole thing. Your choice depends on the size of the bill, the importance of the client to you, and how far you want to press your suit.

As a last resort, you can opt to call your attorney and/or the Better Business Bureau or its equivalent. If your local paper has a troubleshooter column that tries to resolve consumer disputes, present your case and use the leverage of public exposure. If you decide on legal action, make sure the payment will compensate for the cost of doing so and that you can document your claim. Of course, be prepared never to see the client again.

SUMMARY

- Keep accurate and detailed records to account for time and expenses, entering information as you have it.
- Record charges for time and expenses separately and record all business expenses for tax purposes.
- Always ask for and keep receipts to back up expense bills and tax deductions.
- Get sound advice from a competent accountant interested in your business.
- Bill by the project if work isn't continuous with a client and by the month if it is.
- For monthly bills, be consistent about when you send them out.
- Clarify billing requirements with each client and ask how long as you can expect to wait for payment.
- Always keep copies of your bills.

- Try to keep your money out of transactions between clients and suppliers.
- Handle a past-due bill with phone and/or written reminders and press your case further in relation to the value of the client and the amount owed.

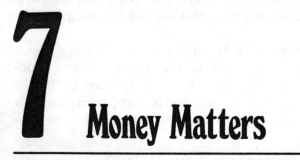

7 Money Matters

No other consideration more clearly separates your freelance business from a pastime than how you deal with money matters. You may like what you're doing as a freelancer, with its independence and other attractions; but at the same time you're enjoying your freedom from the eight-to-five, you bear the burden of financial concerns and responsibilities that are part of any business.

This chapter discusses the money you'll need to get started if you're a beginner and (for those already freelancing, also) what you'll need to keep going. Advice about taxes, licenses, and a personal insurance and retirement program applies to newcomers and seasoned freelancers alike.

FREELANCE BUDGETING

Regardless of the freelance service you sell, you will need working capital to get you started, in addition to sufficient income every month to stay in business. That income must also allow you to put a little aside for more working capital, against the day when you'll have to invest in a new piece of equipment or buy bulk supplies.

If you haven't been working prior to freelancing, your initial freelance income will be a bonus: Nothing plus something equals more than you had. Assuming you have minimal start-up costs (maybe just a few supplies), you will feel on solid financial ground. But once the new wears off and you have become accustomed to a level of income, you will need to pay closer attention to how the money comes and goes so that you can keep up that level.

If before you started freelancing you were getting a paycheck from an employer, you will be very aware of budget concerns because that security is now gone. You will have to finance supplies and equipment for your new business and scurry to close the gap quickly between your last paycheck and your first freelance remittance.

Estimating Initial Costs

Use the following chart as a guide for estimating initial costs of your freelance business. The exact categories will vary, of course, with the service you are planning to offer. "Actual Cost" helps you to check yourself after these one-time expenses have been met. "Date To Pay" gives you a schedule of when you need to have cash in hand.

The cost of several of the items listed is fairly easy to estimate, such as the approximate charge for installing your phone; simply ask your phone company. Rent, utility, and license costs can be estimated by checking the newspaper for office listings,

Initial Expenses

EXPENSE	DATE TO PAY	ESTIMATED COST	ACTUAL COST
Rental deposit on office (if outside home)			
Telephone installation			
Utility deposits			
Equipment rental/ purchase			
Licenses			
Business announce-ment or other initial business development			
Supplies and stationery			
Cushion for un-expected costs (contingency)			
TOTAL			

your electric and/or gas company for utility rates, and city licens-
ing departments for fees. You'll have to take a specific idea to a
supplier for an estimate of other expenses, such as your design
and quantity of stationery.

If you've not yet launched your freelance business, complete this chart now to help you decide about the timing of
your start in relation to when you will have sufficient money.
Also, the total estimate and the schedule for when expenditures
must be made will tell you if, with your current resources, you
can even afford the venture.

Estimating Monthly Costs

The next obvious decision related to money is how much you'll
need each month to meet expenses, as well as your income expectations, and keep up a savings program. A chart similar to the
following one can be useful. Note that, like the guide to initial
expenses, it includes both estimated and actual costs. Complete
such a chart tailored to your particular situation for each of the
first several months you are in business until the items are predictable and you feel you no longer need detailed planning.

Monthly Expenses

EXPENSE	DATE TO PAY	ESTIMATED COST	ACTUAL COST
"Salary" (what you need to meet personal expenses)			
Savings (for yourself and your business)			
Taxes (including Social Security or Pension Plan pro-rated over twelve months)			

Monthly Expenses

EXPENSE	DATE TO PAY	ESTIMATED COST	ACTUAL COST
Preparation of tax return and other accounting expenses prorated			
Office rent (if outside home)			
Supplies not paid for by clients			
Equipment (monthly payment and/or what you need to set aside for future cash purchases)			
Regular outside support (such as clerical)			
Telephone			
Utilities (if outside home)			
Insurances			
Retirement account (contribution and estimated costs prorated)			
Loan payment			
License renewal prorated			
Advertising or other business development			
TOTAL			

Cash Flow

Once you're in business, cash flow will be your primary financial concern. You have to pay the rent the first of the month, even though client checks won't arrive until at least the fifteenth, if then. Also, your car is sure to need a new battery when you least expect it.

Again, your choices for how to regulate cash going out against cash coming in depend on what you're selling and how successfully, the size of any savings account built up prior to freelancing, and your ability to economize. In general, however, you must decide if you will keep yourself solvent with personal savings or a loan until freelance income is sufficient.

Savings will be your choice if

- you have guaranteed business to start or strong prospects within a month or two so that freelance income will be fairly immediate;
- your overhead will be minimal with no major initial purchases so that your need for cash is low;
- your personal expenses can be cut temporarily so that more cash is available to support your business.

Under these circumstances, using your savings account will avoid interest payments on a loan and simplify the financial side of your business. However, make sure that account is large enough to meet *all* your expenses for three to six months in case assignments you had counted on fall through.

A loan will be your choice if

- you don't have any savings;
- you expect to need several weeks or even months to make your business self-supporting;
- you must make major initial purchases;
- you must dedicate savings to meet personal or family commitments that can't be put off.

Even if you feel secure with the size of your savings account and have bright prospects for freelance work, keep in mind that you can get a commercial loan to support your business but not to buy groceries. A savings account with sufficient funds if all goes well is not enough. All may *not* go as you have hoped; so, even if you don't use it, knowing where you can get a loan will allow you to give freelancing an honest try. When in doubt, get a loan. Making those monthly payments can be added encouragement to succeed.

Financial Advice

When you need financial advice, ask your banker. If all you've done is simple transactions, now's the time to find a personal banker and get acquainted because banking may get more complex now that you're in business for yourself. Much like an accountant, a competent and interested banker can be an invaluable support to your enterprise.

Another source of advice is the United States Small Business Administration, the Department of Industry, Trade and Commerce in Canada, or its local equivalent.

Should you need a loan, remember you're talking about a *commercial* loan, not a personal one. The rate should be lower and more money available for such purposes as yours. You may need collateral (such as your car); but the very least you will need is the ability to sell your lender on your chances for success as a freelancer.

You may also be able to get a loan from family or friends. Keep in mind you are funding a business; so deal in a business-like manner with whoever has money to lend. Sign a note, have it notarized, and maintain a complete record for tax purposes of interest paid.

EQUIPMENT AND SUPPLIES

The cost of starting and maintaining your business will be heavily influenced by how much equipment and supplies you need and when. Obviously, the less you have to buy, the more money is available to supplement what may be meager earnings during your early months as a freelancer.

Investing in Equipment

Depending on your service, certain needs will be immediate — for example, you can't make money as a carpenter without tools. To shorten your list of immediate needs, don't buy tools for types of jobs you haven't yet been asked to do. Just know where you can get them and the approximate cost so you can plan ahead. Similarly, your home office may be perfectly adequate with a table reclaimed from the attic, your faithful manual typewriter, and a dining-room chair. As long as you are putting out quality work, you can skimp on appearances (if clients don't come to your office) and, if necessary, sacrifice efficiency for the time being to save money.

For equipment that you must have but can't yet afford or that you will use infrequently, check into renting or borrowing. Some rental businesses offer an option to buy with at least a portion of what you pay in rent applied against the purchase price. In addition to helping with cash flow, renting or borrowing gives you a chance to try out equipment so you can buy wisely later.

You may have time on your hands if your business gets off to a slow start; so use it and your do-it-yourself skills to refinish a desk, build bookshelves, or rewire a lamp for your office. You will save money and be ready when clients start beating a path to your door.

Another way to save on equipment is to use your contacts. Previous work associates, friends, and other freelancers can help you find economical suppliers and even get you discounts. Also, scour the newspaper for sales and private ads for equipment you need. You may find an excellent bargain before you can afford it — but that's when your research into loans can come to your rescue to save you money in the long run.

A telephone answering device will be necessary at the onset of your business if you expect numerous calls that you or another responsible person can't always answer. Don't frustrate your clients by not being reachable or by allowing a child who can't take a message or say when you'll be home to answer your phone.

Installation is simple, and the purchase price usually far less than set-up and monthly charges for an answering service. Some people don't like getting a recording and won't leave messages. However, purchase equipment with quality fidelity and warn clients that you have a recorder.

If you can't stand a recorder and want to spend extra for an answering service, check around about cost, reliability, and courtesy. Ask for references and follow up on them for the opinions of current customers because how your phone is answered is part of your business image.

Investing in Supplies

What supplies you will need and in what quantity also depend on your business and how much money you can allot in the beginning. If you must equip an office with everything from staples to reinforced mailing envelopes, you are looking at a sizable expenditure, say $100. On the contrary, if you can start with just letterhead, envelopes, and business cards, you will spend half that. And you will save even more by substituting quality bond for printed stationery, if the formality of letterhead isn't expected in your kind of business.

For a major purchase of various supplies, contact wholesalers who may sell to an individual, especially if the total cost of your order reaches a preset minimum. Your neighborhood stationer's, drugstore, or discount shopping center can be an economical source for small purchases. Also, if you know someone with an established business, you may be able to piggyback your needs on to a supply order, then reimburse for your portion.

Let's assume you've decided you must have your own letterhead, envelopes, and business cards. Unless you know a printer who will provide them free as an investment in future work from you, ask your associates or other freelancers to recommend a source. Printers specializing in cards may charge less than printers who like larger projects. However, having one shop do both your cards and your stationery can sometimes save you money.

While-you-wait printers may turn out work of sufficient quality for your purposes. Make your requirements and wording very clear, check the type for accuracy and straightness and approve what comes off the press before all the work is done. If you go to such a printer, keep your design simple and use a paper in stock so that the printer is familiar with it. Also, get a supply of blank letterhead paper for second sheets.

Avoid complicated designs that can confuse clients or artwork (such as flowers or cartoons) that can present a less-than-serious image of your business. Regardless of your service, your stationery should sell the quality of your work. When you find a printer, ask for suggestions and look at what other businesses are using. If you know a graphic designer, get advice — or try your own hand if you have design skills.

GOVERNMENT REQUIREMENTS

A major part of your financial homework will be determining how much is due to Caesar and when. Two categories of obligation apply to the self-employed: taxes and licenses required to conduct a business.

Taxes

Discuss this area thoroughly with your accountant when you start freelancing. If you delay, you may face a tax penalty because you didn't act at the right time or in the right way. Your accountant can look at your projected income and deductions to come close to the actual figure due and brief you on intricacies of taxes and the self-employed.

In the United States and Canada, taxes for freelancers are collected quarterly. Thus, roughly every three months, you can expect to pay one-fourth of your total bill for the year. This pay-as-you-go procedure equates to the withholding process used for salaried or hourly employees. The government gets its share as you earn to avoid finding an empty pocket at the end of the year.

Unless you have itemized deductions in the past, you will feel that calculating your taxes as a freelancer is complex. You are entitled to many deductions as the cost of being in business, such as a percentage of your mortgage or rent equivalent to the amount of floor space used exclusively for a home office. Postage, telephone in relation to its use for business, and stationery supplies are other standard deductions. Consult your accountant, the IRS, or Revenue Canada about specific allowances.

Licenses

Another question to ask your accountant or other adviser is what federal, state, provincial and/or municipal licenses or permits are required to offer freelance services in your area. Some licenses have a one-time fee while others must be renewed annually. A business-and-occupation tax may be levied and, with some, you have to pay a minimum tax to keep the license current, even if you have no freelance income to report.

Additional requirements apply if you want to operate your business under a name other than your own. Check with your accountant, the United States Small Business Administration, the Department of Industry, Trade and Commerce in Canada, or its local equivalent. Using your own name may save you a registration fee. However, prospective clients may expect someone offering your service to have a company name — and consider you unstable if you don't. Ask associates, buyers, and other freelancers for advice on this point.

LOOKING OUT FOR YOURSELF

All too many freelancers fail to appreciate the need for a personal insurance and retirement program. As a self-employed person, you have no company medical plan to pay doctor bills, no compensation if you're sick for three days or three months, and no retirement benefits other than Social Security or another pension plan.

To protect yourself, any dependents, and the solvency of your business against a catastrophic loss of time, income, and savings, establish a personal program covering medical expenses and disability as part of your start-up plan. After you're sure the business is viable, add retirement and any other coverage you think necessary.

Medical and Disability

If you are leaving a company to strike out on your own, review its benefit package to see what coverage can be converted from group to individual. You will probably find that at least the medical can.

Weigh its benefits against what is available to an individual on the open market or through a cooperative health service. In Canadian provinces in which a hospital insurance plan is not financed by taxes, self-employed people may be covered by paying their own premiums.

Another method to get medical coverage is to enroll in your spouse's plan. Also, some trade and professional associations offer group medical insurance to their members. *Group* is interpreted by some insurance companies as just a few people, maybe only a dozen; so check out the possibility of banding together with other freelancers for coverage.

Disability insurance will probably have to be purchased on an individual basis. Shop around and make sure agents fully understand what you do for a living and the impact a disability would have, both short- and long-term, on your business. In Canada, a national program of unemployment insurance provides some health and disability benefits.

Retirement

Planning for your retirement may not be uppermost in your mind if you're under forty. Indeed, as a freelancer, you may think that you will never fully retire — and certainly not promptly on your sixty-fifth birthday. However, sock something away. You're not getting any younger, and money stashed in a tax-sheltered retirement account for later use will reduce your tax bill now.

If you are self-employed in the United States, you may establish an Individual Retirement Account or a Keogh Plan, both of which permit annual contributions up to a certain amount or percentage of net income. Taxes are assessed when you withdraw the funds as a retiree; therefore, the rate of taxation should be lower than you would pay now. Such accounts may be set up at a commercial bank, savings and loan, or investment house.

Similarly in Canada, an annual contribution up to a certain amount or percentage of net income may be made to a registered retirement savings plan.

As with other money matters, get advice from your accountant and banker and weigh the services and costs of various institutions offering retirement accounts before deciding where and when to open one.

SUMMARY

- Estimate initial costs to decide when (and if) you can start your freelance business.
- Estimate monthly costs to meet expenses and income expectations and keep up your savings.

- Determine where you can get financial backup if all doesn't go well. Use savings or a personal loan, depending on business prospects, start-up costs, budget flexibility, and availability of savings.
- Call on your banker, accountant, or government agency for financial advice.
- Invest in equipment only as needed and look into renting or borrowing if you can't afford to buy or your need is infrequent.
- Use do-it-yourself skills and your contacts to save on equipment.
- Use wholesalers, neighborhood stores, and contacts to save on supplies.
- Work closely with your printer to get what you want in stationery and business cards.
- Get thorough tax advice from your accountant and expect to pay taxes quarterly.
- Find out what licenses may be required in your area for freelancers.
- Invest in a personal insurance and retirement program to protect yourself and your business and to shelter some income from taxes until you retire.

8 Business Relationships

The various financial considerations discussed in preceding chapters are only one side of the business of doing business. The other is the way you get along with your clients.

Even if you are expert at what you're selling, have thoroughly researched the market, and have devised a comprehensive financial plan to keep yourself afloat, you will not succeed unless you and your clients clearly understand projects and mutual expectations about working together.

This chapter outlines questions for you to ask, ways to put agreements and expectations in writing, and what you should reasonably expect of clients. It also includes suggestions about working successfully with friends, about turning down business for your own good and/or the client's, and about avoiding conflict of interest and office politics.

ASK QUESTIONS

Even though your first contact with a prospective client will probably be written (for example, a brochure or letter about your service), the business "relationship" starts when you make personal contact, either by phone or directly in a meeting to discuss a project. Similarly, the meeting is your opportunity to renew, strengthen, and/or improve a relationship with a previous client. Approach such a meeting as your chance to start a project off on the very best foot.

You'll never know all you need to about the project without asking questions. Even if you were to be presented with what the client thinks is a comprehensive prospectus on the job, you will want to cover any points overlooked and certainly billing procedures.

Don't be afraid to ask. Applicants for full-time positions are often shy about questioning, not wanting to appear too aggressive and fearing to rock the boat. Break this pattern if you expect to be a successful freelancer. Be courteous, of course, and don't pry into areas that have no bearing on your project. But don't be shy. Your performance on the project and your continued relationship with the client are at stake.

Be sure to ask at least the following types of questions.

- What is the purpose of the project; what does the client hope to achieve?
- What is the timing; when will the client be ready to start, and when is the work to be finished?
- With whom will you be working, the client or someone else in the organization?
- Will you be responsible for selecting and supervising suppliers and/or other freelancers?
- What is the project budget? Does that figure include your fee?
- Does the client want progress reports?
- Is your fee (whether by the hour or project) acceptable; what expenses can be expected and covered?
- What is the preferred billing procedure for you, suppliers, and/or other freelancers?
- When can payment be expected; what should you do if it doesn't arrive?
- Does the client want a contract or will a confirmation letter be sufficient?

Experience will teach you other questions important to your particular freelance venture. Your next step, once your questions are answered, is to commit the answers to writing. Contact the client again, should you realize you still don't have thorough information.

With a new and unknown client, your questions may extend to checking that client's reliability. Especially if the project amounts to a lot of time and eventual income, you'll want to make sure that the client has a reputation for dealing fairly and for paying bills. Ask your contacts: colleagues, suppliers, and other freelancers. Call your local Better Business Bureau or its equivalent. If the word on the street is to steer clear of the client, heed it or be prepared for difficulty.

PUT IT IN WRITING

You will be asking for trouble if you come to a verbal agreement at a meeting with a client, then proceed to the project itself without first putting that agreement in writing. All too frequently, the result is misunderstandings about who's responsible for what, deadlines, quality desired, and costs. Even when the verbal agreement itself is quite straightforward, expectations may not be ("I *expected* that you would ask me before going ahead with this part." "But you didn't say, and I just *assumed.*").

Therefore, when you and the client come to terms, put those terms in writing. The degree of formality depends on the magnitude of the project and whether or not you have developed standard procedures from previous experience with the client.

Proposal

A client with a major project may require a written proposal, especially if others are competing for the work. The proposal, then, becomes your opportunity to spell out, in writing, how you would approach the project, your fee and expense requirements, other specifics of the job, and your expectations of the client.

If you have worked for the client before, you may not need as much detail as you would in a new situation. However, don't make assumptions; ask the client what points must be included, especially when your proposal will be reviewed at a higher level by someone you don't know.

From your proposal, the client can understand costs, your method of operating, and what support (such as clerical and photocopying) the client can expect to provide. Your proposal will then be accepted or rejected or a compromise suggested. See Appendix E for a sample proposal.

Confirmation Letter

For small projects or those that have become fairly routine with a client, a confirmation letter should suffice. It spells out

- what the job encompasses;
- due date and other specifics;
- financial arrangement (fee and expenses);
- how supplier bills are to be handled;
- any special assistance you will need from the client.

A confirmation letter should be prepared as soon as possible after you have the assignment, although with a tried-and-true client, you're probably safe in starting immediately with the work. But don't waive the letter unless the client so requests and is willing to assume full responsibility for any misunderstandings. Even in such a situation, write yourself a "memo to the file" that outlines the work, for your own reference.

The timing of misunderstandings usually works against the freelancer in that questions come up *after* the project is done. If someone upstairs balks at paying your bill ("Who authorized this, anyway?"), you can fall back on whatever you have in writing. Should push come to shove (*e.g.*, you take legal action to get paid), your memo to the file may help; but correspondence with the client will be much harder to refute.

Contract

In certain situations, a contract (notarized or not) will be required or desired. Don't be surprised if you see one coming from the client (especially if it's a government project), but ask before you draft one. The formality of a contract can scare someone who isn't expecting you to be so official. A confirmation letter may be sufficient if you know the client. However, a contract requires signatures and gives you extra protection if you have no experience with the client, if the value of the project is high (say $1,000 or more), and/or if you will have to make substantial financial commitments to suppliers on behalf of the client.

A contract should clearly indicate responsibilities, fees, deadlines, and other particulars. If you are selling the same service to all clients, you may be able to prepare a standard document. Sections not applicable to a given job can be crossed out and blanks filled in to fit. Ask an attorney for help if you expect to use contracts frequently.

You are a party to the terms of a contract prepared by a client. The work and the contract may be presented on a take-it-or-leave-it basis; but negotiate any changes you think necessary before signing. If you feel it doesn't cover enough, ask for an addendum or submit a letter to the client confirming your understanding of those other areas.

A sample contract can be found in Appendix G.

WORKING WITH THE CLIENT

As the freelancer coming in to do a job, you are entitled to expect certain things of the client. Your discussion about the work and, to some extent, your written agreement (in whatever form) should cover these expectations, in addition to what the client needs from you.

Meeting Commitments

One of the most discouraging things to any freelancer is having the client frustrate the project by not meeting commitments, while still expecting a quality product, within budget, by the deadline. To do your work effectively and efficiently, you can reasonably expect the client to

- get the project started on time;
- give you advice when you need it that won't be counter-manded by someone else;
- have approvals ready so work can proceed as planned;
- make decisions before a problem gets out of hand;
- stick to specifications if you've made a firm bid on the work;
- pay your bill without delay.

Discuss your expectations with a new client and make them clear as work progresses ("I'll need this draft back from you by next Tuesday afternoon to meet your deadline . . .") Be tactful with all clients, but especially with those whom you hope to see again. As they are entitled to evaluate your work, you are entitled to evaluate how well they uphold their end of the bargain. They may be totally inexperienced with freelancers and require two or three projects to understand how the game is played. If a client doesn't learn and continues to frustrate your performance, take your skills elsewhere. Even if you're paid for the extra time and trouble, such situations often lead to less-than-quality products — which won't speak well of your skill to future clients.

Involving You

You are also entitled to have the client open doors for you to get your job done. If the project requires meeting with other people in the department and/or working with other areas in the organization, the client should make introductions and spell out what your role is.

Don't expect to be treated as an employee — you're not. You're the outside expert and must keep that fact in mind. Employees have certain privileges such as leeway on deadlines and negotiating strength inside the company. They're also automatically invited to the Christmas party and annual picnic. A generous client may invite you, too, but don't count on it. Expect to be involved only to the extent necessary for you to do your job.

DO YOU WANT THE BUSINESS?

From time to time, you will have to decide if you really want certain business and, if so, how you will work with that client. Even when business is slow, don't accept any and all assignments just for the money.

Working for Friends

You can use friendships to your advantage as a valuable source of leads and projects. The pitfall for many freelancers and their friends is that they do not recognize where friendship ends and business begins. You need not avoid working for friends—but do so with your eyes open.

The drawback to mixing friendship and business is that one party can easily and unknowingly take advantage of the other. For instance, the client may assume that, because you're a friend, you will work for less than your current rate. Or you may expect to do the project as you please with no supervision.

To be safe, be as businesslike with friends as you are with strangers. Submit a proposal, confirmation letter and/or contract, just as you would to any other client, and ask questions. You can still talk about old times; but recognizing the business arrangement as such will help ensure that you remain friends after the work is done.

Turning Down Business

Even if you could use the money and know how to do the project, you may be wise to turn down certain business. For example, if you have worked before with a client and experienced numerous and costly problems not of your making, think twice about doing so again. You won't stay in business long if you lose money in such dealings or if you get so frustrated with one client that you can't do an effective job for others. Turn down the project without emotion ("I've gotten away from that type of work" or "I don't think I'm the best person for the job.") A negative remark to a client will never help your business.

Sometimes you will simply be too busy to take on more work and do it well. Most clients will call you again if you decline graciously, and a few may even have the flexibility to delay the project until you can get to it. But if the work must be done now, refer the client to another qualified freelancer if you know one. If you can't vouch for someone's abilities, protect your credibility by not referring.

With your future interests in mind, work out an arrangement with the other freelancer to help out one another in a pinch, but not to take one another's clients. If you don't have such an agreement and you have to refer a client, be prepared to lose the business permanently.

STAYING OUT OF TROUBLE

Two potential hazards to your reputation are conflict of interest and office politics. Recognizing how you can get into trouble will help you avoid these sticky situations.

Conflict of Interest

From time to time, you may be approached by a client's competitor to do some work. Depending on the nature of the project, you could become involved in a conflict of interest that will lose you both clients and jeopardize your reputation as a freelancer.

To protect yourself and your business, determine if the work is really in conflict. Writing sales brochures for Company A and its competitor, Company B, is definitely in conflict. What you know about one clearly influences what you say about the other. However, writing a summary of insurance benefits for both is probably not in conflict because that information is fairly standard.

Ask yourself which is the more valued client when you have to make a choice. If Company A gives you lots of business and Company B proposes one project only, your choice will probably be to remain loyal to Company A. When in doubt, discuss your quandary with your original client. If the client sees no conflict, proceed with the new work and signal immediately, should a problem arise.

Office Politics
Another source of conflict is the office political environment. As a freelancer, you may come and go frequently and even take advantage of clerical support, the photocopier, or postage meter. Depending on your business, you may be around the office a lot and need to be on friendly terms with employees.

Keep in mind that you are there because the client considers you an expert at whatever you do. You have been brought in either because no one on staff can do the work or because someone on staff is incompetent. Especially in the latter case, feelings against you can run high.

To maintain your credibility with the client, complete your work with a friendly but aloof attitude. Don't be another branch on the office grapevine or another spoon stirring the rumor pot.

SUMMARY

- Start off a new project by collecting all the information you can, including (with an unknown client) a check of references.
- Clarify agreements in writing at the onset of work, using a proposal, confirmation letter, and/or contract that spells out the project.

- Discuss with clients what you expect of them in the way of approvals, staff support, introductions, and other such needs.
- Cautiously mix business and friendship by recognizing where one ends and the other begins; always work with friends in as businesslike a manner as you do with strangers.
- Don't be afraid to turn down business that will be more trouble than it's worth.
- Refer any business you can't handle to another qualified free-lancer, rather than take on more than you can do competently and on schedule.
- Ask yourself in a potential conflict-of-interest situation if the work is really in conflict and which client is the more valued. Always be aboveboard when such a situation arises.
- Be friendly with employees in a client's office but avoid office politics.

9 The Work Environment

Regardless of the type of freelance service you provide, you'll want a work environment that's convenient, pleasant and, above all, conducive to working. Experience on previous jobs should tell you in general what you need and enjoy in your surroundings; so now that you're in control, convert that experience into your own freelance office.

This chapter looks at these options for your office: at home, in rented or leased space, or in one of several alternate locations. It also offers advice on maintaining the integrity of your office, wherever it is, and of your work schedule.

YOUR OFFICE LOCATION

Your needs for space and equipment will, of course, depend on your type of business. At the very least, you'll do bookkeeping and billing and file your records. Your needs may also be quite complex, such as a large space with a certain type of lighting, movable partitions, public access, and room for equipment. Based on whatever your needs are, determine the best location for your office.

At Home

Early in your business and perhaps as a permanent location, consider setting up your office at home. With increased transportation costs and appreciation for the pleasures of integrating work with other activities, working at home is appealing to more and more people. A home office will be your choice if any of the following circumstances applies:

- You can conduct your type of business at home.
- You have sufficient, pleasant, isolated space available at home.
- You want to keep down costs.
- You can work alone.
- You have other reasons for being at home.

Consider an office at home if your business is such that you can conduct it at home. An office in a residential area is feasible if clients seldom, if ever, need to come to you. For example, if you are a freelance writer of fiction articles, you will work primarily by mail and phone and could operate quite conveniently out of your home. If you are a photographer, on the other hand, and expect clients to come to your studio, you will want it readily accessible; therefore, a home office probably isn't your choice, unless you live in a small town.

Consider an office at home if you have ample space of the right kind. In general you will want your office in a pleasant location separate from normal household activity. A basement corner, spare bedroom, or isolated nook can be adapted well (assuming you don't have the luxury of adding a room to meet all your specifications). The space required may be only as large as necessary to accommodate your desk, additional storage, and perhaps a typewriter.

Space at home will not be appropriate if it is in a main thoroughfare or if it is in a dark area that you won't find pleasant to occupy. Remember that you may spend several hours a day, including night and weekend time, in your office and will want it situated to meet this need. It should be dedicated space—something that says, "This is an office." A sewing area in the utility room or corner next to the television isn't an adequate setup.

Consider an office at home, even if it doesn't fulfill all your requirements, if you want to keep down costs as you start your freelance business—or permanently. With a home office, you are entitled to a tax deduction for the space (instead of deducting what you would otherwise pay in rent). Also, a home office drastically cuts transportation costs because you aren't commuting to work, and you can even save money on clothing because you don't have to get dressed up if you're staying at home.

Consider an office at home if you can work well alone, away from the interplay of coworkers found in a regular office situation. As a freelancer, you'll have to watch the tendency to become isolated by your workstyle. To get the inspiration and cross-fertilization of ideas that you need to avoid stagnating and still work at home, go to trade or professional meetings and have lunch with colleagues to help keep in touch.

Consider an office at home if you have other reasons for being there. If you have children who need attention, a retired spouse who would appreciate your company or simply the desire to get away from the office-tower crowds, you will find working at home an advantage. Indeed for many people, such an environment is one of the big bonuses of freelancing.

Rented or Leased Space

If none of the above circumstances is true for you and you don't want or can't have an office at home, look at what space is available to rent or lease. Such an office will be especially appropriate if

- clients must come to you;
- a business address will help establish your credibility;
- you prefer to get away from home to concentrate on business.

Consider a rented or leased office if clients must come to you to conduct business. You will want them to find you easily, maybe from external signage. You will also want them to step into a pleasant and well-appointed space that is dedicated to nothing else. With an office outside your home, you are fully in control of what they'll find.

Consider a rented or leased office if your type of service requires a business address. Your credibility may be enhanced by your location, and clients will assume you are well-established just by the address. This point is one you should check out as you research prospects for freelance success. Ask buyers of your type of service what they expect. (Chances are, they will emphasize the quality of work, rather than where it is generated.)

Consider a rented or leased office if you prefer to get away from home to a space that is clearly your own, without the distractions of children, chores waiting to be done, or door-to-door sales people. Also, some freelancers still want the discipline of going to work, and space outside the home can meet this psychological need.

If you're just starting out and don't have extensive physical needs, see what is available on a rental basis. As a one-person operation, you will more likely rent with a month-to-month rental agreement. This arrangement gives you the flexibility of moving if you need to on short notice, without the restraints of a lease. The advantages of a lease, however, are that it ties down monthly payments for a specified period in an escalating market and assures you of an office on a long-term basis. You may remodel or otherwise change the space under either arrangement, although as a renter, you can expect to do the work yourself.

One possibility for lower-cost office space outside of your home is a cooperative office in which you rent or lease your space and share with other tenants a common reception area, switchboard, and duplicating center. This option will be especially attractive if you need such services but can't afford to buy them entirely on your own.

If you want an office outside your home but your business doesn't require that it be centrally located, look into what suitable space is available in your neighborhood. Being located close to home (without being home) will save you time, transportation costs, and the higher cost of prime space downtown.

To find out what is available, check with your banker, accountant, other freelancers and associates, or scan the newspaper ads. Although realtors tend to concentrate on larger space than you will probably need, they are another source of information.

Alternatives

One option if you must do concentrated work at a client's office is to ask for space there for the duration of the project. You will still need room elsewhere for bookkeeping and storage; however, you may not need a formal office setup as long as the project lasts. Large businesses often have a spare cubicle or room, and clients can appreciate the advantages to them of having you on premises to do your work effectively.

Another choice on a start-up or interim basis may be borrowed space. Here your contacts might lead to someone willing to let you set up shop in a corner of a large office. For example, a friend who owns a business may have extra space you can use with the stipulation that you release it on demand. Or a neighborhood church or other building may have an empty room. If you know an apartment owner with several vacant units, see what you can negotiate. Such an arrangement would have to be temporary — but may be quite adequate to help you get started.

Especially important if you choose one of these alternatives is to make sure clients can easily reach you by phone and mail. You will be behind if, to save money, you lose jobs because clients couldn't contact you.

MAINTAINING THE INTEGRITY OF YOUR BUSINESS

A full-time employee for a corporation has a clearly defined office and certain hours during which work is expected to be going on. As a freelancer, *you* are the one to establish such discipline. If you don't, work won't get done on time and, if you're constantly interrupted, it won't get done well.

If you work at home, family members must understand that your space, equipment, and supplies are not for everyone to use. A lock on your office door and labels on your scissors and tape dispenser may be in order, especially if some of the supplies on hand belong to clients.

Decide what kind of environment clients should find if they come to your office—and make sure they do. You may even need to ask your neighbors for help if your office is at home; a barking dog next door won't bring clients back when they need your service again.

Maintaining the integrity of your time can be more difficult at home than at an outside office. Impress upon yourself, family, and friends that you are not at home to do the laundry, help with homework, or entertain the neighbors during your working hours. Some interruptions may be tolerable; but distractions have to be kept to a minimum if you are to be effective. As much as you can, organize your day to accommodate all nonwork activities into blocks of time (such as first thing in the morning and again in late afternoon). Reserve all other time for work.

One way to make your needs clear is to call a family council to explain your requirements. Keep family members up to date on your projects to help them appreciate why you need your own time and space. Invite friends and neighbors to an "office" party to state in a pleasant way that you are definitely serious about your business.

Working at home evenings and weekends (which may be required) puts a further demand on your organizational abilities. One help will be planning ahead as soon as you know you will have to work during what for everyone else in the house is free time. Another aid will be your spouse and/or older children to take on more of the load at home when you simply must work.

SUMMARY

- Consider having your office at home if you can conduct your business at home, have the right kind of space available, prefer a tax deduction to paying rent and want to keep down other costs, can work well away from associates, and/or prefer to be at home for other reasons.

- Consider rented or leased space if you can't have a home office, have clients who will come to your office, must have a business address to establish credibility, and/or can concentrate better away from home.
- Alternative office locations might be on client premises or borrowed space from another business or neighborhood building.
- Make sure clients can reach you by phone and mail, wherever your office is.
- Maintain the integrity of your space, equipment, and supplies by making sure family and friends appreciate their purpose.
- Maintain the integrity of your time by keeping distractions to a minimum and scheduling and negotiating work time that is not to be violated.

10 Subcontracting for Services

On occasion, you may get involved in a project which you can't do alone. Or the client may want you to handle details that require working with suppliers.

In such situations, you will need to call in help from another freelancer for particular expertise or an established business for supplies or services. This chapter offers advice on selecting freelance talent and suppliers and how to be a successful intermediary between your client and such outside help.

SELECTING FREELANCE TALENT

The shoe is on the other foot when you must select freelance talent to supplement your own. In doing so, you shift from seller to buyer — and your success in making this switch has a direct influence on your credibility with the client and on your prospects for future work. Following are suggestions about when to recommend using additional freelance talent and what to look for.

When To Use Extra Talent

Like so many other points covered in this book, the decision about when to turn to additional freelance talent depends on your kind of business. If you offer yourself as a "full-service" freelancer who does a project from A to Z, you will seldom look for other talent. You have built your business on doing the whole job and will have to come through on your own. Exceptions are when you have an unexpected surge of work which you still want to handle or when an emergency (such as illness) requires you to find a substitute to keep a project on schedule.

If, on the other hand, your freelance service covers only one part of a project (for example, the landscaping of a home but not the construction of brick walkways), you may frequently be in a position to subcontract for other talent. You have built your business on a particular skill and do not sell yourself as able to do every part of a big project.

Also, you might work with someone else, at the request of a client who wants a project done faster than you can do it alone or who wants to give a friend or relative an opportunity to work with you for the experience. Under either circumstance, confirm with the client that you are the "prime contractor" with the responsibility of coordinating and decision-making.

What To Look For

Your first consideration will be to find another freelancer who can do the job well and on time. Your credibility as the person doing the subcontracting is on the line; so put quality ahead of loyalties to freelancers you know, including friends.

Your second consideration will be to find someone whose method of operating is compatible with yours and with what the client expects. If you're highly organized and like to have a detailed schedule for doing your work, don't subcontract with another freelancer who is entirely the opposite, even if the end product is satisfactory. If the client expects close attention and a result exactly to specifications by the deadline, make sure the freelancer you select can meet this expectation.

A third consideration is cost. You and the client may work out cost estimates before you find another freelancer to help. That person must fully understand the requirements and be willing to meet them within budget. Even if the client has no set figure for the other freelancer's fee, determine an approximate limit so you won't propose someone who will work for twice what the client had in mind.

Do not exclude a friend from consideration as the other freelancer, but make sure the friend meets the above criteria. Interview the person you select much as you would a prospective employee, if you don't know the quality of work already. Ask to see samples, as appropriate, and check references. Brief the client on the freelancer's background and skill, prior to the final selection. Leave that decision up to the client, even if it's yours by default ("Go ahead and get whoever is best . . .") As a freelancer, you should not be expected to bear the burden of such a decision. How the budget is spent should be left to the client, with the benefit of advice from the outside expert.

SELECTING SUPPLIERS

For a major project requiring supplies and/or services, you could be asked to manage the entire process. The client may not know what to do — where to go for materials or production to augment your work. Or the client may know that a better product will result if you work with suppliers with whom you're already familiar.

As soon as possible after you get a project, recommend suppliers to the client so that you have plenty of time to get a decision and schedule your job. Look for suppliers who can provide what's needed on time and at the price quoted. Ask around if you haven't worked with a possible supplier because you can't afford to lose your good standing with the client if a supplier lets you down. Make sure a supplier agrees to the billing procedure preferred by the client. Alternate methods are discussed in Chapter 6.

ASSURING CLIENT SATISFACTION

Credibility is a primary consideration in any subcontracting situation. As the one in the middle managing the project, you have responsibilities not only to the client but also to the other freelancer or a supplier involved. Don't get so involved with the project that you neglect details that will help ensure client satisfaction.

Client Approvals

Once you realize that a project will require other talent and/or suppliers, verify as part of your contract or confirmation letter the extent to which the client wants to be involved in the process. The range can be from "Keep me well posted" to "Just send me the bill."

Protect yourself by putting the onus on the client to review qualifications and cost estimates before you make a commitment to another freelancer or a supplier. Also, be certain what contact, if any, the client expects to have with the other freelancer or a supplier. If the project is a brochure to explain a new product, for example, does the client want the design proposal to be presented by the designer or want to check press proof at the printer's? Such requests may feel like infringement on your territory; but the client is entitled to infringe to any degree. They'll probably drop off as your credibility builds.

Managing a Subcontract

Be as businesslike with the other freelancer or a supplier as you are with the client in spelling out requirements and expectations. You are the buyer and should behave like one by making sure all agreements are clear, preferably in writing. If you work a lot with another freelancer and have a "master agreement" about fee and areas of responsibility, you won't have to detail your arrangement each time you cooperate on a job. Because supplier bills can be high, get estimates on paper for every project, even if they're only notes from phone conversations with a regular supplier, and put those estimates in writing to the client.

Clarify with both the client and the other freelancer or a supplier your role as intermediary. As the manager of the project, assume responsibilities to which that label commits you. For example, make sure you are in a position to approve work before it goes on to the client. Also, ensure that any criticism by the client is channeled through you to the other freelancer or a supplier so you can work out problems.

As discussed in Chapter 6, set up a billing procedure that is agreeable with all parties. As also advised, try to keep your money out of it.

SUMMARY

- Turn to another freelancer when, because of workload, you need someone else to take over part of a project or when, because of an emergency, you need to keep a project on schedule.
- Make sure at the onset that you are the project manager.
- When looking for other freelance talent, consider competence and ability to work on schedule, compatible method of operating, and cost.
- Select suppliers early, leaving the final decision to the client. Consider competence, price, and ability to deliver on time.
- Establish and maintain a system for client approvals, clarify roles in the project, and agree to billing procedures.
- Put agreements in writing and take your job as project manager seriously.

Appendixes

APPENDIX A—SAMPLE COVER LETTER

Sharon T. Lawrence, President

Lawrence Enterprises

1 Industrial Way South

San Marie, California 35270

Ms. Lawrence:

The enclosed information summarizes my services in an area more and
more organizations such as yours are emphasizing--that of solid
communication planning.

My interest is in developing a master communication plan that will
assist Canton Manufacturing to meet profit and image objectives in
the short- and long-term. I am aware that your organization has had
considerable growth during the past year, as well as changes in staff.
In such an environment, responsible planning is critical.

I can appreciate that you have many demands on your time. If you
care to suggest someone else with whom I can talk, please do so.
Otherwise, I will call you the week of February 1 to see if you share
my opinion that a meeting would be mutually beneficial.

Sincerely,

Dwight G. Evans

Enclosure

APPENDIX B--SAMPLE SUMMARY OF SERVICES

When To Have a Communication Program

A well-conceived program should be considered when rapid growth begins to tax existing communication activities and to require different systems, rather than simply an expansion of current ones. A communication program can help if, for example:

- putting out fires is becoming time-consuming and an inefficient use of resources;

- senior management and staff members are losing touch with one another;

- one-on-one communication within a diverse company no longer provides all the timely, accurate information needed;

- training activities are hard-pressed to keep up with corporate needs;

- increasing sales require more output from a larger organization while maintaining the quality and personal involvement of a small organization.

Having a communication plan doesn't automatically mean dozens of new and expensive activities. It does mean, however, doing what you do effectively and efficiently.

How I Work

My job is not to change what you've been doing for years, usurp the position of communication personnel, or jeopardize your agency's contract.

As a consultant, I provide an outsider's view, as well as specific expertise with no obligation for a long-term association with your company. Also, I put forth a concentrated effort without disrupting on-going activities.

To help you look at needs and ways to satisfy them I start with a comprehensive audit of your communication requirements through interviews, surveys, and critiques of past efforts. From this research, I come up with a clear statement of where you are today with your various publics. In this process, I work with any communication person(s) on your staff and/or your account executive.

Then I put that statement alongside existing activities and projections about the future of your business, see how they match up, and recommend changes. I next compile a comprehensive report and explore with you approximate costs and a timetable for implementation. I also can assist you in this latter phase, if necessary, and follow through with an evaluation once your program is fully in place.

Every step is outlined for your approval before any work is done, including preparation of a written contract. My job is completed when you accept the final report, unless we agree that I can be of further assistance.

My Qualifications

For the past four years, I have worked with various organizations to provide programming, management, and editorial expertise. I started my career ten years ago after completing a master's degree in journalism.

I am experienced in researching, budgeting for, staffing, and evaluating a communication program; supervising personnel; writing; editing; and producing a variety of print and audio-visual materials for internal and external audiences, and working in diverse management environments.

In addition, I remain professionally active to provide clients the most current approaches, including participation as a workshop leader at professional association conferences.

APPENDIX C--SAMPLE PERSONAL LETTER

Pat L. Carey, President

Canton Manufacturing, Inc.

701 S. Harvard St.

Trinity, Ohio 72163

Pat:

As we discussed at Leonard's gathering last week, I am interested
in talking with your Personnel vice president about the employee-
orientation project you outlined.

You know my work and, if you feel my expertise may be what is
needed, I will appreciate the referral. Then your vice president
and I will see what we can work out.

Thanks for your assistance,

Felix Anderson

APPENDIX D--SAMPLE BILL

John S. Simpson, Office Manager

SIMCO Engineering, Ltd.

4431 Marrian Boulevard

London, Ont. N6A4N7

Mr. Simpson:

This letter confirms our agreement of August 30 regarding typing of
the Overlake report.

You will retain my services at the rate of $7 per hour for typing, as

Appendix D (cont.)

well as correcting of typed pages. The schedule calls for rough copy
to start coming to me on September 8. The approximate date for proofed
and changed pages is September 24.

For this project, I will coordinate with the project director. Upon
completion of the work, my itemized bill will be sent directly to you.
My estimate of the time required is fifteen hours and I will let you
know immediately should the project appear to require more time.

Thank you for contacting me. I look forward to helping you complete
a well-done report.

Sincerely,

Carrol Tall

APPENDIX E--SAMPLE PROPOSAL

Paul Cathay

Vice President, Personnel

Canton Manufacturing, Inc.

701 S. Harvard St.

Trinity, Ohio 72163

Mr. Cathay:

This proposal is submitted to meet your requirement for development
and implementation of your company's employee-orientation program.

I propose to start with a meeting with you and any others you think
appropriate to draft our planning objectives, a process that will help
me focus to the best advantage on your needs and restrictions. Once

those objectives are approved, I will move into an analysis of your
present orientation process, including the following steps:

1. Discussions with members of the Personnel staff currently
   involved in orientation.
2. A review of activities, including any supervisory training
   that relates to employee orientation.
3. Discussions with selected employees who have been with the
   company for less than a year.
4. Discussions with selected supervisors about their present
   role and perceptions of the need.

Based on this research, I will draft objectives for the program and a
suggested schedule of activities, including specific elements, responsibilities, budget, and time requirements. Once you have accepted
that draft, I will proceed to finalize a budget and implementation
schedule.

Because the time needed to implement the plan will depend a great deal
on elements of the program, this proposal must be limited to an estimate for the planning only, up to the point of implementation. Based
on my knowledge of the company and this type of project, I propose to
complete the planning phase in twenty to thirty hours, at a rate of
$30 per hour. My schedule will permit me to start on the work within
two weeks of a signed contract.

Thank you for the opportunity to submit this proposal. I look forward to working with you and hope you will call if you have questions.

Sincerely,

Felix Anderson

APPENDIX F--SAMPLE CONFIRMATION LETTER

John S. Simpson, Office Manager

SIMCO Engineering, Ltd.

4431 S. Marrian Boulevard

London, Ont. N6A 4N7

Mr. Simpson:

Following is an accounting of hours by date spent typing the Overlake
report, at $7 per hour.

September 8	Initial typing	4.5 hrs.	$31.50
September 10	Initial typing	2.0 hrs.	14.00
September 11	Initial typing	3.5 hrs.	24.50
September 26	Corrections, changes	2.5 hrs.	17.50
September 27	Corrections, changes	2.0 hrs.	14.00
		14.5 hrs.	$101.50

I hope you will call when I can be of assistance again.

Sincerely,

Carroll Tall

APPENDIX G--SAMPLE FREELANCE CONTRACT

_____ hereby retains the freelance services of _____ for the following projects:

1. _____

2. _____

_____ is responsible for providing products of the quality desired according to schedule within cost estimates submitted and is further responsible for advising the client in advance of any necessary deviations in schedule or cost.

The client is responsible for supplying all necessary information, for timely decisions about the projects and for providing whatever staff assistance may be appropriate.

Terms of this contract are that services will be provided at an hourly rate of $ ____ from initiation through completion of the projects. Contact for the client is _____ who is responsible for approving all plans and estimated expenditures on behalf of the company. A bill detailing hours by date and activity performed will be issued at the end of each month (starting _____) and will include an accounting of all expense items. Payment will be expected within thirty days. Mileage will be charged at $ ____ per mile, and any purchases on behalf of the client will be approved in advance and billed at cost.

This contract can be reviewed at any time by either party and shall be in effect until satisfactory completion of the projects.

_____   _____
Freelance signature   Client signature

_____   _____
Date   Date

Index

A

Accountants, 75-76, 93
Advancement, 8
Analyzing the market. *See* Market
 analysis.
And Associates form of business, 3-4
Annual reports, 36
Approaching prospective clients,
 40-43
Associates, determining market
 potential and, 31-32
 See also Contacts
At-home office, 110-12
 family members and, 114-15
Avoiding problem conditions, 23, 27

B

Better Business Bureau, 81, 99
Bids, 61-62
Billing clients, 77-81
 methods and requirements of,
 77-79
 past-due bills and, 80-81
 sample bill, 126-127
 supplier charges and, 79-80
 written agreements and, 101
 See also Bookkeeping
Board of Trade (Canada), 36, 57
Bookkeeping, 72-76
 accounting advice and, 75-76
 receipts and, 75
 setting up, 72-75
 See also Billing
Brochures 42-43
Businesses, established. *See*
 Established (competing)
 businesses
Business relationships, maintaining
 good, 98-107
Buyers of freelancer services:
 determining market potential and,
 31-32

determining your rates and, 59
See also Clients

C

Career advancement, 8
Cash flow, 88-89
Chamber of Commerce, 36, 57
Charging. *See* Rates
Classified ads, 35
Clients:
 approaching prospective, 40-43
 billing, 77-81, 101
 competing with established
  businesses and, 45-46
 conflict of interest and, 105-6
 expectations you have of, 102-4
 finding sources of, 30-38
 follow-up with prospective, 44-45
 maintaining good business relationships with, 98-107
 mix of, security and, 50-51
 raising your rates and, 65-67
 repeat business and referrals from,
  47-49
 researching prospective, 35-38
 subcontracting for, 118-22
 See also Buyers of freelance
  services
Competence, 13
Competing with non-freelancers,
 45-46
Confirmation letters, 101
 sample letter, 129
Conflict of interest, 105-6
Consistent rates, 64-65
Contacts:
 determining market potential and,
  31-32
 maintaining files on, 38
 as research sources, 37
 word-of-mouth recommendations
  from, 40-41

Contracts, 101–2
  sample freelance contact, 130
Covering letters, 41–42
  sample letter, 124

D

Deductions, 93
  record keeping for, 74–75
Department of Industry, Trade and
  Commerce (Canada), 75, 89
Detachment, 8, 11–12, 103, 106
Directories, 36
Disability insurance, 94–95
Drawbacks of freelancing, 9–12

E

Economic survival, 9
Economy of hiring a freelance, 46
Editorial services, 59
Education, 20–21
Effectiveness, developing security
  and, 50
Efficiency, 13
  developing security and, 50
Emotional insecurity, 10
  weathering slow times, and, 51–52
Employers, former, 33
Employment, part-time, 3, 35
Enjoyment in your work, 22, 25
Equipment, investing in, 89–91
Established (competing) businesses:
  competing with, 45–46
  determining your rates and, 59–60
  finding clients and, 33–34
Estimates, 61–62
Expenses:
  budgeting start-up and monthly,
  84–89
  chargeable, 68
  documenting, 72–74
Experience, 5, 21, 24–25

F

Family members, maintaining the
  integrity of your business and,
  114–15

"Feast-or-famine" syndrome, 10
  See also Slow times
Fees. *See* Rates
Files, maintaining, 38
  See also Records
Finances, 84–96
  budgeting expenses and, 84–89
  income taxes and, *see* Income taxes
  investing in equipment and supplies
  and, 89–90
  license requirements and, 93
  personal insurance and, 94–95
  retirement plans and, 95
Financial data on prospective clients,
  36–37
Flexibility, 6, 15
Follow-up with prospective clients,
  44–45
Freelancers, other:
  determining market potential and,
  32
  determining your rates and, 58–59
  finding clients and, 34
  referring work to, 105
  subcontracting, 118–20
Freelance services (freelance
  businesses)
  buyers of, 31–32, 59. *See also*
  Clients
  determining your, 20–28
  financial requirements of, 84–96
  selling your, 14, 40–53
  sources for finding clients for,
  32–35
  summary of, 125
  types of, 4–5
Freelancing:
  definition of, 2–4
  determining your prospects for
  success, 12–17
  drawbacks of, 9–12
  maintaining good business relationships and, 98–107
  objectives of, 5–9
  security and, 9–10, 49–52
  weathering slow times and, 51–52
Friends:
  working for, 104
  subcontracting, 119

H

Health insurance, 94-95
Home office, 110-12, 114-15
Hourly rates, 60-61

I

Income potential, 6-7
Income taxes, 92-93
  at-home office and, 111
  deductible items and, 74-75, 93
  receipts for, 75
Independence, 5-6
Individual Retirement Accounts, 95
Insecurity, 9-10
  weathering slow times and, 51-52
  See also Security
Insurance, health and disability,
  94-95
Integrity of your business, working
  at home and maintaining, 114-15
Intensity of work, 11
  See also Involvement
Internal Revenue Service, 93
Involvement, 22, 26
  maintaining, 8-9
  See also Intensity
Itemized statements, 79

J

Job evaluations, 22
Job hunting, freelancing as aid in, 9

K

Keogh Plan, 95

L

Letters:
  confirmation, 101
  personal sales, 43
  samples of, 124-30
Licenses, 93
Listing services, 34-35, 58-59
Loans, 88-89

M

Managing yourself, aptitude for, 13
  See also Efficiency
Mass mailing, 44-45
Market analysis, 30-38
  of potential for your service, 30-32
  research sources for, 35-38
  of sources of actual clients, 32-35
Meetings, billing time for, 69-70
Mistakes, 69-70
Motivation, 14

O

Objectives of freelancing, 5-9
Office politics, 106
Office space, 110-116
  alternative, 115
  at-home, 110-12, 114-15
  maintaining integrity of your,
    114-15
  rented or leased, 112-13
Other freelancers. *See* Freelancers,
  other
Overload, handling, 45-46

P

Part-time employment, 3
  classified ads for, 35
Past-due bills, 80-81
Performance:
  evaluations of, 22
  record of, 21, 25
Personal letters, 43
  sample, 126
Problem conditions, avoiding, 23, 27
Professional association(s), 49
  directories, 36
  listing services of, 34-35, 58-59
Promoting your freelance service. *See*
  Selling (promoting) your freelance
  service
Proposals, 100-1
  sample proposal, 127-28
Pros and cons of freelancing, 5-17

Q

Qualities of a freelancer, 13–15

R

Rates, 56–70
  additional charges and, 67–70
  consistent versus variable, 64–65
  determining your, 56–60
  methods of applying, 60–65
  raising your, 65–67
Receipts, 75
Records, maintaining, 72–75
  of contacts, 38
  See also Bookkeeping
References, checking new clients',
  99–100
Referrals:
  from clients, 47, 49
  from contacts, 40–41
Refusing work, 104–5
Rented or leased office space, 112–13
Repeat business, 47–49
  raising your rates and, 66–67
Researching prospective clients,
  35–38
Respect, 7–8
Responsibility, 10–11, 14
Resumés, 41–42
Retainers, 63–64
Retirement plans, 95
Revenue Canada, 93
Rush jobs, 45–46

S

Salary. *See* Rates
Salary surveys, 57–58
Savings accounts, 88–89
Security:
  developing, 49–52
  loss of, 9–10
  retainers and, 63–64
  weathering slow times and, 51–52
Self-analysis, 14
Self-evaluation:
  for determining your freelance
    service, 22–28
  of qualities as a freelancer, 12–17

Self-motivation, 14
Self-responsibility, 10–11, 14
Selling (promoting) your freelance
  service, 40–53
  approaches for, 40–43
  aptitude for, 14
  competing with non-freelancers
    and, 45–46
  follow-up for, 44–45
  referrals and, 40–41, 47, 49
  repeat business and, 47–49
  word-of-mouth and, 40–41
Skills, 4–5
  how others see your, 22, 26
  maintaining and expanding, 49
  primary, 20–21
  secondary or weak, 23, 26–27
Slow times, weathering, 51–52
Small Business Administration, 75, 89
Small businesses, 3
Society of Certified Public
  Accountants, 76
Speculation, working of, 62–63
Statements, itemized, 79
Switchboard as source of
  information, 37
Subcontracting, 118–22
  client satisfaction and, 120–22
  freelance talent, 118–20
  suppliers, 120
Success:
  determining your chances for, 12–17
  prior record of, 21, 25
Summary of services, 41–42
  sample letter of, 125
Supplementing your income, 6–7
Supplier charges, methods of billing,
  79–80
Suppliers:
  finding clients and, 33
  subcontracting, 120
Supplies, investing in, 91–92

T

Telephone answering device, 91
Time:
  chargeable, 67–68
  documenting, 72–74
  nonchargeable, 69–70

Trade association(s), 49
  directories, 36
  listing services of, 34-35, 58-59
Training, 20-21, 24
Travel, 68-69
Turning down business, 104-5

U

Unemployment, freelancing during
  periods of, 9

V

Vacancies within businesses, 34
Variable rates, 64-65

Variety in work, 7, 51-52
Volunteer projects, 49

W

Word-of-mouth recommendations,
  40-41
Writer's Market, The, 59
Written agreements, 65, 100-2
  subcontracting and, 121-22
Written sales material, 41-44

Y

Yellow Pages, 37

A GIFT FROM
ADVENTIST DEVELOPMENT
AND RELIEF AGENCY
P.O. BOX 60808 - WASH., DC 20039

IN COOPERATION WITH THE PUBLISHER

NOT TO BE SOLD

A GIFT FROM
ADVENTIST DEVELOPMENT
AND RELIEF AGENCY
P O BOX 60808 - WASH, DC 20039

IN COOPERATION WITH THE PUBLISHER

NOT TO BE SOLD